REUNION

LOVE POEMS TO THE MASCULINE & FEMININE

AN ANTHOLOGY

FLOWER *of* LIFE PRESS

Praise

"Spirituality can be found within every creative art: dance, painting, singing, sculpture, storytelling and of course poetry. Sacred Reunion is a gorgeous creative healing poetic response from many different hearts to our cultural stories and myths of pain, suffering and separation. Poetry is the perfect medium to counter such stories. Poetry is a great stream of light contributing to the spiritual revolution occurring across the planet right now!"

—Steve Ahnael Nobel, Author, dreamweaver, and creator of The Soul Matrix

"Rebecca has created a body of work that is both human and divine. The exquisite collection of poems speak to a longing that must not be squashed but instead inflamed and embodied. The tone and presentation of this work is both sublime and inviting, reminding us once again, of the essential presence of the feminine, in surrender to the unknown depths of Love. Delicious, through and through."

—Anaiya Sophia, Author, Storyteller and Mystic, www.anaiyasophia.com

"Sacred Reunion: Love Poems to the Masculine and Feminine is a heartfelt collection of poetry that speaks to our common humanity—our passion, our need, our wounds, our healing. These intertwined conversations about love offer timely insights both inside and outside of our own experience."

—Annie Lampman, author of Burning Time: Poems (Limberlost Press) and the novel Sins of the Bees (Pegasus, New York)

"As the known world around us falls, the poetry in Sacred Reunion touched the deepest sweetest place in my soul giving me courage to know the true revolution is within us and it is coming."

—Phoenix Na Gig, www.goddessrocks.co.uk

"Sacred Reunion is a breathtaking and gorgeous collection of poetry that carries deep medicine for the heart. I was touched by each entry and could feel the divine energies of each poem weaving together as a magical tapestry. The words come alive and as the reader, I could feel them imprinting into my being. This book will speak to the parts of you that want to experience love, connection and divinity. I feel so blessed to have read this gift."

—Asha Frost, Indigenous Medicine Healer

"A beautiful invitation to bridge the gender-ation gap, after centuries apart! Reading this book softens the heart's edges and invites a deeper relational healing. If we don't heal gender, we don't heal anything. This book is a sweet step in the right direction."

—Jeff Brown, Author of An Uncommon Bond and Grounded Spirituality

"I felt transported into the heart of love and awakening that was being fully expressed from both the male and female poets, in this beautifully written anthology. I loved the journey of both call and response from the masculine to the feminine bringing me deeper into my own longing through the words so heart-fully expressed. I invite you to take your time in savoring this book.

It will sit on my bedside table so I can read it again, and again, finding my passion renewed and my heart lifted. The eloquently written poems are pearls of wisdom, to help heal your heart and expand your capacity to love and be loved. Thank you Rebecca Cavender, for hearing the 'call and answering it.'"

—Diana DuBrow, Scent Priestess of the Emerald Temple

"This collection of love songs is a refreshing and much needed immersion in memories of what love feels like. Called home to our own heart's yearnings and celebration, each poem is a new experience that awakens us to love again. In a world which sometimes forgets the sacredness of the Divine Feminine/Masculine union, we sense the presence of the energy that gives life to everything that exists everywhere. This is a precious gift. Receive it often!"

—Linda Lee, Bishop of the United Methodist Church, retired

"What struck me as I read through this beautiful anthology was the very visible blurring of lines: which was masculine and which was feminine? Revelation: the heart knows no gender. We love, adore, and worship the beloved. Just so.

Coming at these deeply felt tributes to the beloved from a feminine perspective, I was enraptured by the deep spiritual love of the masculine—a love that matched the feminine every step of the way.

And perhaps this is why the placement of the poems works so perfectly: poems in couples: the masculine—the feminine. At times, I had to ask myself: which is which?

Congratulations to Rebecca Cavender for being inspired to write this book. I suspect it will be healing for many; inspirational for many more."

—Goody Niosi, Author

"Sacred Reunion is a journey through loneliness, grief, longing and peace into re-union, joy, passion and sensuous dance through poetry. It is a call to a love that complements the feminine and the masculine. It is recognition of what has taken us away from one another, and now returns us to ourselves and one another in partnership and harmony. We have journeyed alone. Here is a sacred, honoring path to journey together."

—C. Christy White, Poet, President of Arizona State Poetry Society, MA in Creative Writing: Poetry

"This anthology is an immensely healing and inspiring thing to read, and I imagine to write and make: looking at both the internal balance of masculine and feminine, anima and animus, as well as the external. The very premise of the project is one of understanding, insight, empathy, a meeting and reaching in, out and across. Without names and biographies, you won't know which poems are from which genders. When you close the book, the pages kiss."

—Anna Maria Selby, Poet

"*Rebecca Cavender has created the Yin and Yang in the poetic form. A revolutionary conception that connects the masculine and the feminine in a divine anthology of love. Healing, empowerment, nurturing and respect of one soul for another—total and exquisite balance and harmony. I know of no other collection, religious or spiritual, which so beautifully unites this cosmic duality. This volume of searingly touching verse serves to reunite the divine masculine and divine feminine with words from the heart.*"

—Olivia Beardsmore, Founder of Burning Woman Festival

"*Each of these poems, vibrant, subtle, and uniquely textured, weave together a warm tapestry that ultimately tells a story we all long for, of union, merging and love—a return to our very origin. Beautifully rich and multicultural. Wrap it around yourself and rest in remembering.*"

—Lisa Schrader, Coach and Founder of AwakeningShakti.com

"*In a time of great reconciliation between the masculine and feminine archetypes, these gentle words offer a balm for the soul, easing the pain we have yet to heal.*"

—Sam Peret, Founder of Heartwise

"Sacred Reunion *is an intimate dance of the voices that reside in our hearts while calling forward the deepest yearning of all: to find the healing within and remember that we are whole—neither male or female, but a sublime alchemy of both.*

Each offering in this book coaxes us to hear our inner female and our inner male selves as they coyly come out of hiding to embrace each other, understand, forgive, and heal all that has been hurt; and in its place, yield a great beauty: that of the breath of reunion!

Do yourself a favor...get your favorite drink, light some candles, get comfy, and dive in. Let this anthology take you."

—Elayne Kalila Doughty, Ordained Priestess, Psychotherapist, and Founder of the Priestess Presence Temple

"It's been a long day. My legs hurt from a workout. My body is heavy. My mind tired from the day's work. As I open up this book of poems, there is a quiet anticipation. Of what, I am not sure. The journey perhaps; poetry is about the journey. I read a line, then another. My body softens a bit. The edges slowly melt. My soul stirs. Time slows down as I drink in each word.

Art like this is an invitation. It beckons us, asks us to hear another's heartbeat and to remember our own. Sacred Reunion, in particular, is one beautiful love letter—to men, womxn, humanity, ourselves. It invokes. It stirs. It lays out love and lust and romance and hope and the messy, complicated, gorgeous dance between the masculine and feminine. What a dance it is.

At a time when many of us long for more communion, with others and our own spiritual center, the raw and tender words living in this book give us a way to do just that. Settle in, after a long day or a long year. Grab a glass of wine or pour yourself some tea and let your heart break open. Let it heal and feel and remember what it is to love."

—Christina Dunbar, Storyteller Stage-Actress and Facilitator to Creatives, Creator of RED, an LA workshop for female artists, www.christinadunbar.com/red

"In these divisive times, Sacred Reunion: Poems to the Masculine & Feminine is a reminder to honor, balance and integrate our uniquely female and male energies within us and to know that our healing with each other first begins with our own self-healing. What a beautiful balm and path to love."

—Holly Payne, internationally published novelist of Damascena, The Virgin's Knot, The Sound of Blue, and The Kingdom of Simplicity

"What could be more nourishing for a world often feeling divided than a call to union? Not just a call, an offering. A ritual act and offering of creative initiating a call and response to one another. Much has been said on the topic of love and writing about love—yet as we change as a people and evolve, the narrative changes. This book is a step in the changing narrative of union."

—Shiloh Sophia, Founder MUSEA : Intentional Creativity®

FLOWER *of* LIFE PRESS

Sacred Reunion: Love Poems to the Masculine & Feminine
—An Anthology

Copyright © 2020 Rebecca Cavender

Book design by Astara Jane Ashley, floweroflifepress.com

To contact the publisher, visit floweroflifepress.com

Library of Congress Control Number: Available upon request

Flower of Life Press, Old Saybrook, CT. 06475

ISBN-13: 978-1-7337409-9-9

Printed in the United States of America

Beloved of my eternal heart, I leave this
offering to you:

I sway for you;
hips, an oceanic welcome
the embrace of home,
the taste of remembrance.

Consumed with the Pulse of Life,
my feet become drums,
a beckoning rhythm.

Palm on womb,
eyes alight,
blazing into yours
I reach for you,
Open
a surrendering passion,
an invitation of return to

Our balance:
a bright-dark dance of
Cosmic Love.

©Rebecca Cavender

Table of Contents

CHAPTER 1 ~ *The Call of Love* 1

CHAPTER 4 ~ *The Revolution of Love* 115

Foreword

JIM BODEEN, POET

Sacred Reunion is a poetry anthology not looking away, but into, a collection of poems not content with the conversation that's out there; and editor, Rebecca Cavender, wants her poets and their poems to be heard. She's their herald, the conductor bringing the music.

Sacred Reunion is not content with perimeters.

Another poetry anthology?

Sacred Reunion is the anthology claiming cosmic consciousness.

Human beings here to have a divine experience. Poets with resumés witnessing their love.

All poems are love poems; don't we put them in the bin with political poems? There best be some play involved, or I'm not interested. There's play in these poems.

These poets put their words on the daily doorstep. Open the door and what's there? Hands on love. Words not turning away from daily work, inter-action and inner-action.

Four chapters on love. Call, nature, song and revolution. That's the claim of editor Cavender.

In her Preface, Rebecca Cavender welcomes the reader by stating that the anthology comprises men writing poems of adoration to the feminine and women writing poems of adoration to the masculine, adding that our consciousness depends on finding balance of the masculine and feminine in each of us, that moving forward depends on re-assimilation.

How about that—poems of adoration.

Cavender calls this anthology a "unique call & response, a collaboration." Echoes of praise spirituality from African-American churches.

Cavender has paired poems with poets who did not know one another, hoping to engage, to reach out in hope. Only a few poems were intentionally written to an unmatched pair of poems.

Erin Hawkins writes in "Letter of Love":

In refuge you rest.

> *medicine and meaning*
>
> *mending and maturing*
>
> > *you grow.*
>
> *Only to return to the fight again.*
>
> *I stand in sacred witness...*

Lee Amburgy's "Love Letter" claims "...every time a first time... beautiful as if it were your name..."

One of my favorite poems, Jon L. Napora's, "I Push the Limit", is written in couplets. Napora's last couplet quietly reads: "I do not care / You're on my mind," then waking us with a stanza break and last line, "You are my mind." New territory.

Let him take some time to assimilate that.

Sarah Eden Davis breaks ground in her title: "I Went Into the Great Below."

Felipe Roberts' poem, "The Air is Tight", begins repeating the title in the first line: "The air is tight./It strums like a chord/half-tuned/ during dawn somewhere/I wake, hummed to life/by the chill."

His poem works its way through noise and waking… "always the connoisseur of rolling notes/and tingsha bells…" returning to the beginning in his final lines: "Might as well tighten the air/and burn it all/a broken banjo/silenced by too much talking."

Heenal Rajani's poem, "Creating the Story", insists on one thing in different ways, "We will not be filtered…"

Part invitation, part play, Marie Mbouni is present, not tipping her cards, in an almost conventional first stanza image: "Content/I watch you/watching me," before coming out in the second stanza, catching her lover "…gazing at Mama Ocean/…Open the door to my water…"

She'll nurture her lover, but she'll "please myself" receiving cosmic aid from stars and moon doing the real work.

"Welcoming the Masculine Home", Mbouni again, becomes yoni, portal, gateway…unstruck sound/the darkness…calling the lingam Hindu phallic symbol through the waves in a tango.

Rebecca Cavender, editor, mystic nurse of these writer/lovers earns her street-cred stripes in this stanza of her final poem, "Wind Songs":

This love nourishes the dry landscape of

of any body that has been

over-watered,

under-heated.

John Beckett writes in "Two Minutes":

For just two minutes

I want to love you

In silence.

The writers are fresh. And yes, they're fresh, too.

Nomita Khatri asks, in "Speak To Me":

In dappled shade

In the shadow of the rock.

Reading through the poems, taking notes, going back, going on, trying to find Cavender's threads, I begin to get it, too.

Cavender's not asking the reader to read, she wants us away from the laptop, eyes and toes dancing together, moving. This grouping of poems wants a language experience with the body.

This is the transportation she's after. She's got it. I put the notes down. I start over.

Can one do that, and get it right? One can do that. *Sacred Reunion* does it.

One better at you. Do that. Move.

How did she do this? Cavender, I mean. How did she put this together? Oh. Okay. I see.

Re-union. Union in real time. In a polarized time. Polarizing, Climate change. Permafrost. Ice-breaking heart-melt.

Work your way through the world. This is your life many-themed. What you gonna do when the well runs dry? Dance papa-sanh, get up and dance. Be with the one you brought. Body-up.

Receive your way through these poems, receiving. Give and take.

You say you've been giving more than you've been getting back. Are you getting back everything being sent your way?

Maybe you got something you want to listen to again.

About your love. Yes. That. Holding on? Holding on. How long do you think you can do that?

—Jim Bodeen
7 February 2020

Foreword

AURORA SUNU, POET

A NOTE ON MY HOLY QUEERDOM

As someone who identifies as queer, I had some misgivings about offering into this project based on the adoration of the masculine and the feminine being bodied and gendered between male/female, and perpetuating a mythology that is the unspeaking of so many.

However, I believe that Rebecca Cavender, the writers, and indeed the beloved readers, are in a space where it is truly possible to envision the varied and infinite possibilities of the expression of masculine and feminine as the sacred union within each of us.

Certainly, my intention—and part of my life's purpose—is to create space for the reclamation and restoration of the sacred feminine within us all.

However, I deeply believe that the conversation that this book opens is a much-needed healing for many—individually and collectively.

The reunion of the sacred masculine and feminine is a long overdue prayer that is, in part, seeking us as much as we are it.

This body of poetry is an essential part of the ongoing dialogue that must be had around our language, expression, and the creation of our experiences—of our humanity and our divinity, and our walking as love…as individuals and as a collective.

I place my own offering here as an altar space, knowing that love is never done; love simply does not know how to confine its utterances. Love, much like language, is in a constant state of flux, an ever-changing animal. Love is a river in a perpetual propulsion of expansion of source...of becoming and unbecoming. It is life force itself, with which we, as humans, get to co-create with—imagining and reimagining; silt for our fertile living.

Love Always,

Aurora Sunu

Preface

REBECCA CAVENDER

Welcome to this poetic anthology comprised of men writing poems of adoration to the feminine and womxn writing poems of adoration to the masculine.

The healing between the masculine and the feminine must occur for us to truly move forward in the world, for us to continue here as conscious beings.

Each of us have been hurt by the imbalance between us.

We have been distant from one another for too long.

Our society, culture, myths, history, and power dynamics have kept us apart.

We need to create something better for the children of our world.

And I believe, with all my heart, that the possibility for a new way exists.

Because…we belong to each other…and to ourselves.

What better way to forge this path, than through the written word?

Why not write letters, poetry, prose, stories to one another?

THE INSPIRATION

The inspiration for this anthology came to me, suddenly, while I was driving along dark, windy, Northern California roads in 2016, returning home to Washington State, after spending time with a beloved mentor, Diana DuBrow, who taught me the ancient art of anointing.

Anointing trained me to remember we are whole. That our bodies are sacred. To feel the kiss of love upon our skin—in service to love, in service to union.

This ignited a fire within me to help reunify the hearts of men and womxn…the reunification of *all people—regardless of gender, which is not binary.*

Immediately, it was clear to me that this project wanted to take on a life of its own and be an anthology that included diverse voices—voices that bring us back to the poet's heart…the heart that sees all people, all life, all experiences as art. As beauty. As love.

While I envisioned this clearly and knew exactly how the book would be structured, The Muses took me on a personal, initiatory journey to prepare me. To ready me. I had to go back into the fires and forge a pathway to my heart.

It took another two years before I was ready to ask others to collaborate. Two years of healing some of my past trauma—including sexual abuse and domestic violence at the hands of men—and open my heart to feel worthy of truly receiving love…even if just from myself.

Upon reflection, how could I write a book about (re)union when I still needed to stitch and mend some of these frayed pieces back for myself? I couldn't. Not with integrity.

During this time, I tended my burning heart, began recognizing my inner beloved, and healing the wounds between myself and the masculine.

All along, I did what all poets do: Listen. Listen to feel when the timing is right…for a poem, for a letter, for digging deeper…or in this case, to ask others to collaborate on a beautiful, ambitious, healing project. I waited. I healed. *I was readied.*

Eventually, my life partner arrived on the wings of an answered prayer—after six years of being single.

Our union sparked another initiation: the fruition, the birthing of this book.

One summer day, standing in his bright kitchen on the edge of the Salish Sea, my partner inquired if I had any incomplete projects that I felt passionate about. My bones began to tremble and tears rushed to my eyes. Goosebumps pricked my skin.

The pounding of my heart let me know that it was time to bring *this book* to life.

It was time to call in the poets.

THE POETS

What mattered to me was raw, genuine, provocative, enticing, sensual writing from individuals who felt passionately about healing the wounds between the masculine and the feminine. The tone needed to be intimate. Inviting. Honest. Not academic. Not perfect.

I made a list of people I thought might want to join. A list of those I'd hope would join. A blank space open for the mystery to reveal, in its own time, people who were driven toward unity. People who soaked in words. People who loved to write. Those who knew words could be medicine.

It was clear to me that there would be a unique configuration of people called to this transformative anthology. Each person who said yes awed me. I admired their audacity to take committed action toward actively healing collective wounds, through words.

Poets, artists, mystics—we've always been the revolutionaries, the culture stirrers, the change-makers.

It's time for a new revolution.

I'm humbled by each writer and their faith in this project—one unlike any other that I'm aware of: I do not know of an anthology written by both men AND womxn for the explicit purpose of reuniting us.

What a powerful offering to share with the world!

DIVERSITY/INCLUSION

This anthology aims to be inclusive. The diversity of poets includes unpublished and published neurodiverse writers from different countries and various ethnic/racial, spiritual, educational, abilities/disabilities, genders, sexuality, socio-economic backgrounds and other identifiers.

A NOTE ABOUT MEN/WOMXN & MASCULINE/ FEMININE

It's important to note that whilst part of the mission and purpose of this anthology is to create healing between the masculine and feminine, it could appear, due to the language used, that it is for cis-gendered, heteronormative people. This is not the intention.

It is my intention that this project provides enough healing to open the door to greater, more inclusive/expansive conversations and re-unioning that go far beyond gender...

Yet, we have to start somewhere, and this is where I needed to begin...

A steppingstone into the river of love.

We're interested in healing the masculine and feminine *energies* that are within each of us individually and collectively (which is not about gender or gender specific roles, despite the language).

Even beyond *this,* it's my belief that there is a union of these energies that, when merged, creates something neither masculine or feminine—yet also NOT, not masculine and feminine—but a sacred third.

This anthology was written to *re-union* all of us...to heal our hearts, to heal separation, to heal our world, to revolutionize love *for all beings.*

From this perspective, this project is for all people, regardless of gender or sexual identity.

THE COLLABORATIVE PROCESS

Because this book is really about the reunification of divine love within us all, I knew, to ensure the integrity of the book's purpose, it must be a collaborative creative process based on true community, at whatever depth each individual wanted to participate.

From the outset, each poet was invited to co-create and become involved in our micro-community. This included live, online intuitive writing circles that I guided so they could receive a spark of inspiration for their poems; in fact, many of the poems from the chapter, *The Song of Love,* come from one of these writing circles. We also had several video chats and a private online group to discuss the progress of the book, including how we wanted to publish and market it.

THANK YOU FOR JOINING US IN THIS SACRED REUNION

This is your gift. This is your call.

We are on the forefront of a new shift.

Will you join us? Will you devour the divine love letters? Will you taste these poems? Will you remember that we are One?

Let's bow to the divine in one another, see each other's nobility, honor our differences, and kiss the light between us, in acts of forgiveness.

...That is where this book was birthed from: A desire for us to re-member one another and love one another. To heal the old wounds that separate us and keep us in toxicity, distrust, and mistrust.

I hope that you join me in this journey of remembering love. True Love. A True Love that lives within our pores, in the soles of our feet, in our very bones. A True Love that connects us to the Wise Ones of Old, to our Creator, to the Divine in All, to ourselves, and to one another.

May you meet us there.

—*Rebecca Cavender*

Acknowledgments

I would like to thank each of the courageous poets who contributed to this powerful anthology. I thank you for trusting the process, trusting the mission of the project, trusting your soul. My heart is full of gratitude. Your spirit, love, art, words, energy, hope—and in some cases, financial contribution—have created this book of poetic prayers. Thank you for trusting me to shepherd it through and being by my side, all along. You are amazing.

I humbly give thanks to the training, mentorship, and love of Diana DuBrow, as it is through my anointing training with her that the inspiration for this anthology was born.

I am grateful for the experiences where I've felt separation and loving bliss from the masculine; the extremes brought forward the fruits of desire to feel an ecstatic union and surrender to my inner-masculine and, ultimately, with a beloved.

David Lea-Smith, my husband—you've been a consistent light, walking beside me, holding me, accepting me, teaching me to trust myself and love—thank you.

My daughter, Freya—may you go forward in this world knowing less separation between not only men and womxn—and whatever societal constructs those mean, but don't really mean—but a wholeness within you and all beings…a wholeness that sings of harmonious beauty.

Jeff Volk—thank you for volunteering your time and editorial expertise to several poems. I am grateful for your consistent support.

Heenal Rajani—thank you for helping to create and participate in this anthological community. Your ongoing support and dedication to serving our Earth in all her forms has been an inspiration.

I am deeply grateful for Flower of Life Press and our wonderful publisher, Astara Jane Ashley. Thank you for feeling the beauty of this anthology, designing, and publishing it so its message can be shared. Thank you for believing in this book of love. I love you, sister of my heart.

To all my incredible teachers and mentors (Elayne Kalila Doughty, Ariel Spilsbury, Jim Bodeen, Asha Frost, Bridgette Doerr, L'Erin Alta, Jacqui Wilkins, Diana DuBrow) and soul brothers and sisters—Thank you for your influence, support, and devotion.

My ancestors and the poetic ancestors of us all—I am humbled by your guidance and the legacy you leave as traces of love within us.

And finally, to you, dear reader: Thank you for being here. Thank you for being a divine lover.

How To Experience This Book

A NOTE ON THE BOOK'S ORGANIZATION

UNIQUE CALL & RESPONSE

I knew when the idea for this book came to me, that each poem would be a call and response. I wrote to the potential authors:

"In my bones, I know that the perfect authors will collaborate on this project…and that whatever is written by the men/womxn will end up, naturally, being a call and response: I see that what one man writes will match what one of the female authors wrote…and that they would then be next to one another in the book."

The book is a collection of conversations—of aches, of yearnings, of pain, of ecstasy, calling to one another…responding to one another. The call is answered and echoed back with each poem. Thus, poems are to be read in pairs. They've been matched, as they speak to one another.

The poems are alive and speak for themselves.

With only a few exceptions, the poets with paired poems did not know one another. Only a small handful were intentionally written as a response to an 'unmatched' pair; most pairings occurred naturally.

Once they were all collected, a pattern emerged—a natural story was told. Patterns became themes, which became the chapters in the journey of love.

THE CHAPTERS: A MAP

This poetic anthology is organized into four chapters. The chapters tell a story from the *Call of Love* to the *Nature of Love* to the *Song of Love* and, finally, leading us to the *Revolution of Love*—which is our destination.

The chapters are a journey in love. Start at the beginning.

Each poem appears in order, very consciously, to guide you through the heartbreak, the separation, the yearning of love…to the primal experience of how we are love, expressed through nature…to how we join in harmony, singing our songs…eventually reaching the ultimate hope: a revolutionary love, a sacred (re) union and remembrance that we are merged as one.

The book, as it is composed, is a map of love.

May you enjoy the journey and revolutionize love…

Love Letter

TO THE READER

Dearest you,

Here we are. Connected. A web-matrix of love, of eternal embrace, bringing us closer.

We have been distant from one another for too long. We have reached for the other—tips of fingers, barely touching—in hopes of grasped hands, in loving reunion.

Our world has kept us apart: Myths and legacies of betrayals; currents of mistrust; fear of being secretly reviled; imbalance of power.

The pain has scorched across wild fields, destroying forgotten vows of honor, devotion—noble hearts.

There was a time we danced the erotic dance of life: the fire within us, emboldened through the Flame of Love and ecstatic union.

Do you remember?

We are being asked to come together again in penetrative receptivity.

We are being asked to heal the wounds that have separated us—the Masculine and the Feminine.

We are being asked to find sanctuary in one another's arms and feel the hush of forgiveness brush across our lips and hearts.

Will you bow to one another?
Will you kneel in adoration?

Will you see the old ache held in the bones we've carried?
Will you set it free?

It is time.
It is time for us to clear the veils and blow away the mist.
Take my hand as I anoint you with a kiss.

Let us find our way to one another through words of divine love, harmony, and restoration.

I see you.

Dear reader, I know you are a Divine Lover. And as such, an eternal beloved of words, letters, poetry, art. Of all things beautiful.

Welcome.

—*Rebecca Cavender*

Will you bow to one another?
Will you kneel in adoration?
Will you see the old ache
held in the bones we've carried?
Will you set free the Call of Love?

—Rebecca Cavender

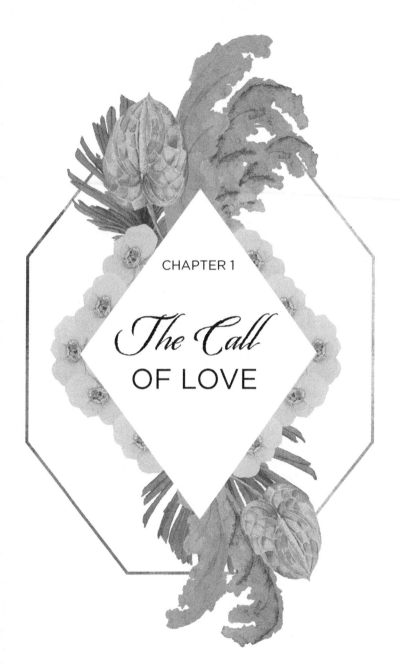

CHAPTER 1

The Call
OF LOVE

The Letter of Love

I Need You.
       fire and flood
       guts and glory
             you are.
The world pursues you
       hunting and hungry
       irrational and incursive
             you rise.
You move with the indwelling of the great warrior spirit.
       jumping and jabbing
       kicking and knocking
             you act.
Moving life itself with your pain and power and purpose.
You are tired.
The weight of being when the dogs are at your heels is a
sun with 10,000 rays penetrating body and soul.
listless and leery
languid and lethargic
       you retreat.

Come let me be your peace, kiss your brow, soothe your pain.
In refuge you rest.
     medicine and meaning
     mending and maturing
          you grow.
Only to return to the fight again.
I stand in sacred witness, whispering in devotion.
I Need You.

©Erin Hawkins

A Call for Revolution

This is a call for revolution!
>Let this be the generation that finds the solution.
I believe in you.
>>You are my hope for humanity.

In this world of separation and conflicts
>let us seek union,
>let us find peace,
>>let us topple the walls of shame
>>that have been erected in our minds.

Everything that divides belongs to the past—
digital culture has no borders;
love has no borders.
>Let us be rebels for peace,
>warriors of the heart.
>>This century will be the century of peace
>>or else humanity will cease
>>>to exist.

Bring on the revolution of compassion.
May women lead all the nations of the earth.
67 billionaires (all men) grab as much wealth as half the
earth's population:
pathological individualism
codified in the fabric of our society.

Let us make use of our collective intelligence.
Let us be the generation that acts—
humanity is our family,
the world is our home.
And you...

You resonate with the solar system,
the Milky Way and the cosmos—
way beyond anything you could imagine.

Practise compassion like an Olympian.
Let empathy be your driving force.
As life rocks you, let yourself sink and flow.
Everything that is broken can be fixed.

Make love your language—
a million quiet revolutions.

©Heenal Rajani

Fences

1.
To build the bridge, we must tear down this fence.

You say you don't like fences.
I say I do.

Fences make me feel safe, hidden.
They make you feel cut off from
enjoying others, robbed of spontaneity.

Fences let me avoid what I fear.
I fear communion.
Communion leads to broken hearts.

I say I'm happy being alone inside my fenced garden.
It's beautiful and wild in some places; neat and tidy in others.
It's how I like it.

(Do you approve?
I might give up a part to gain approval from you.)

2.
Please, love me for who I am.
Accept all of me:
my fences might open

But,
They protect you from me.

I am blunt, harsh, insensitive at times.
Oblivious to your feelings.
I poke at you with my words.
I go too far: you retreat, hurt.

We return back to ourselves.
Gates close, lights out
weeds grow in the path between us.

3.
I sit in my lovely garden
alone
content in the river of sovereignty.
My garden thrives.

Yet,
a desire, a seed finds its way through the fence,
making a ruckus
messy and complicated,
even in the dark earth.

©Deborah Wood

The Mystery of She

What if she says,
all of the days that we had
Turned from the Wow! to the So...then the Bad?
What if I failed,
got myself nailed in this try.
Would it be "fuck you my dear" and goodbye?

Would it be good,
if I understood an ambiguous mood?
Flowers in bed, cards gladly read, love, wine and food?
Would I be like him,
The one she lets in after a storm?
Gives me a seat, something to eat, wrap me up warm.

Where is the key, to her love,
to be found?
Is it just me who can't see the profound.
In this mystery,
the mystery, of she.

Can I just be me,
easy to see, nothing to hide?
no marvelous skills, craving for thrills or swallow my pride.
I can only give the life that I live, that truly is me.
If my person is
not her perfect bliss, am I missing that key.

Still in her bed,
loves me she said, soothing my fear.
Making her smile,
still for a while am I here.
Searching the key,
deep inside me, hard to reveal.
Has to be found, deep in my ground, that is the deal.

Where is the key, to her love,
to be found?
Is it just me who can't see the profound.
In this mystery,
the mystery, of she.

©*Stig Olsen*

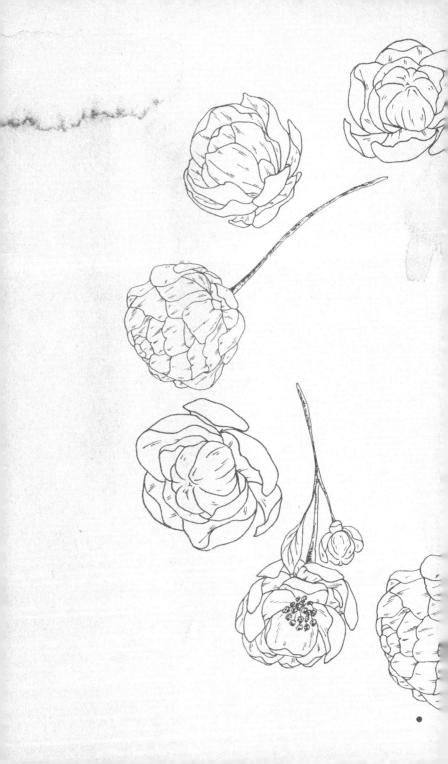

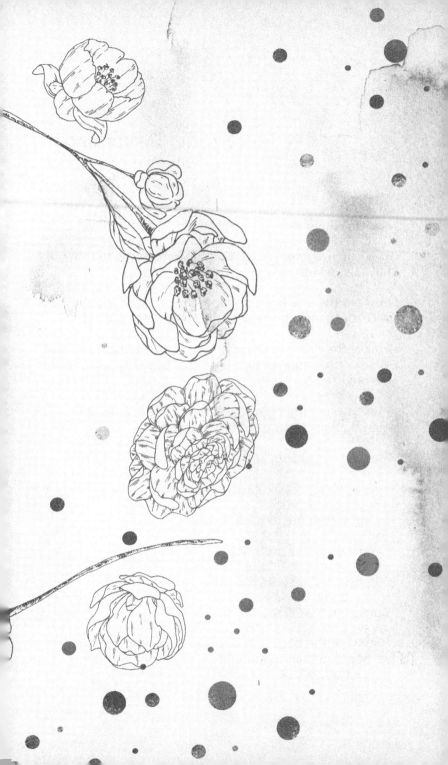

A Love Letter/Soul Swimming

Dear Lover,

You are the one.

The one I've chosen. To wake up with in the morning. To fall asleep with at night.

You are the one I rest my head upon. The one who I travel with, both inside myself and outside in the world.

You're the one whose breath I breathe in the morning. Whose heat I feel at night. Whose heavy exhales I hear before I sleep.

I say you are my soulmate. When I see the depth in your eyes, I could swim in it for an eternity.

My soul sees yours and your soul sees mine.

Yet, when I see the burrow in your brow, the one that tells me of your aches,
I want to bring you back to life.

I know you have suffered.

Too much, too soon, too fast.

Sometimes we fight.

You want the bedroom door open, so you can hear if someone breaks in at night.

I want the bedroom door closed, so it's just us, without distractions.

You tell me I grew up sheltered. You grew up with gunshot.

I wish I could love the fear out of you.

I long to be closer to you in the safe haven of our souls.

I feel you seeing me to the core.

This my love, is the only safety I've ever longed for.

Trust me. I will tell you what I need.

Come closer, my love.

Death will always be there. Waiting for us.

Let's take this borrowed time in our bodies and make love to life itself.

I'm here, waiting...

To hear your voice hum through my bones on the dance floor.

To feel the warmth of your chest against my cheek.

To be aroused by your firm fist grabbing at the roots of my hair.

To sink into our dreams of boundless life together.

To you, my love, I say: Let's bow down to life and death.

To you my love, I say: Let's sink into the mystery of love.

With love,

Your Lover

©*Krista Kujat*

My Love Letter to You

Waking beside you, inhaling the scent of your hair tucking behind your ear kissing the tender sensitive curve.

Morning coffee and your smile, that sigh with your first sip.

Showering with you, washing each other calling you beautiful as though it were your name.

Telling you midday I'm thinking of you, daydreaming of coming home, kissing your smile, caressing your ass every time a first time.

Sharing our days over a glass of red, you in my lap, hands held because there is never enough touch.

Laying with you, in the dark, the night bearing fruit of our desires.

Waking to your beauty my sunrise writing this love letter anew.

Morning glow awakens him in the confines of their comfortable room.

He lays quiet, eyes open to the possibilities before him.

She lays next to him; beautiful raven hair, creamy skin, pink lips always curved in smile, and breasts any man would enjoy.

He traces her body with a light feathery touch not wishing to disturb, simply wishing to soak up her beauty with his fingertips, to mounting delight of his queen, by her king.

©Lee Amburgy

I Want to Feel You Stronger

My heart is anchored in the holy land.
I want to speak to you.

I tell the stories of ancestors, of my body, of
drumming in my ears,
head in sacred waters.

I hear you.
Come closer.

Heal me with your heartbeat that drums through the cells
of time.

Cry me.
Cry our tears of the years.

Stand with me as I rise in you.
Dance with me as I snake through you.
Sing with me as my voice opens you.

I want to feel you stronger.

©Deborah Wood

I Push the Limit

To you ; for you
I cannot bring myself to wait

I push it to the limit
for you

I recall your stare
as we laid together

side by side
my muscles ache

I do not care
You're on my mind

You are my mind.

©Jon L. Napora

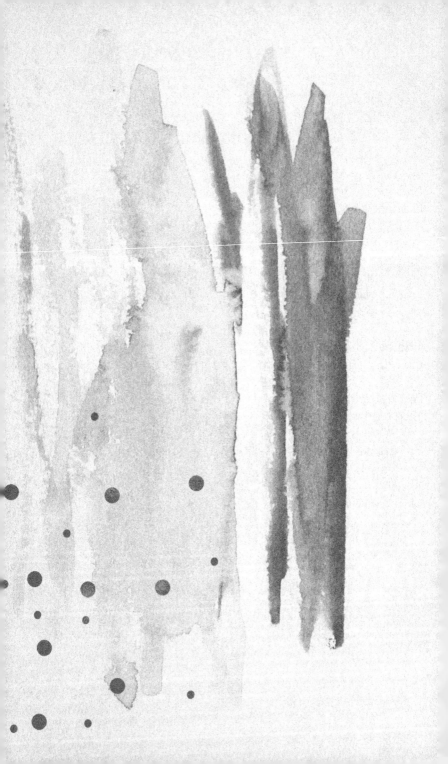

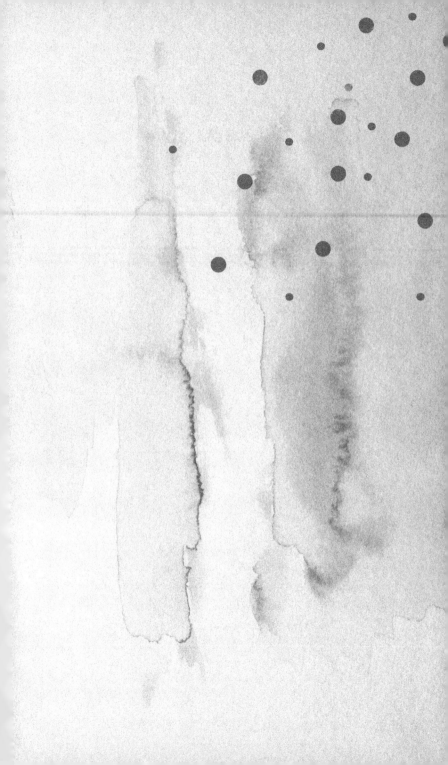

Dearest Love

for so long I have felt you
searching
        calling
        crying
        longing

falling and rising
through the ages

I cried with you
        dancing
        dreaming

Inhaled your scent
a breath of life
        at the edge
        of the infinite

You were always waiting
to feel the power
        of my heart
        beating through yours

I was always ready
to move beyond longing
        into
        being

with you

two faces
of one truth
        now, finally, you
        are ready too

So slowly
we rise
        and fall
        together

Into each other
hearts beating
        pulsing
        laughing

United
as one
        forever
        again

©Satya Colombo

I Went Into the Great Below

to bring all parts of myself back home:
Those lost children,
scattered voices—scared and hiding in
dark tunnels,   quietly

inside my cells,
a lineage of pain,
          —black hole sun caved inward with
          punishment
          aching and longing,
their whispers of anguish, cries of disconnection
calling out, the destruction of man.

"Please, spark a fire in your heart
to find us here and bring us home.
We long for your holy touch."

All joy stolen, I walked with sunken chest,
grasping fleeting pictures—
dreams of love far away outside myself
until I anointed my heart and
opened the petals of this flower
to reach him
to touch him
to love him

to forgive him

I sang softly to him
vibrations of fire, love, rage
pleasure, pain
expanding this flame.

I surrender, I trust:
I give my body to this song of reunion.

©Sarah Eden Davis

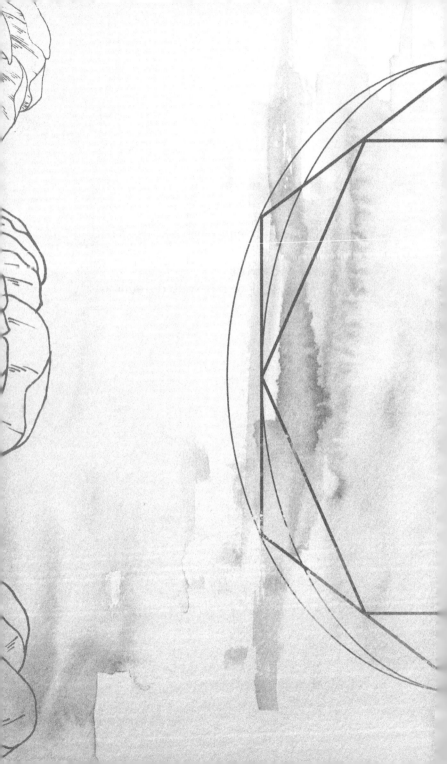

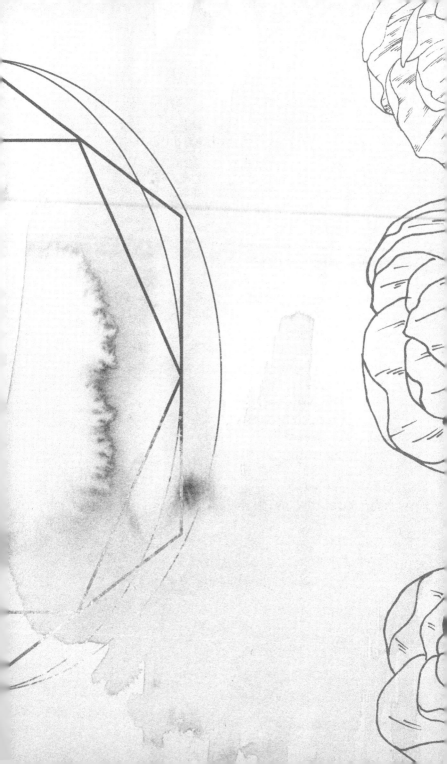

The Air is Tight

The air is tight.
It strums like a chord
half-tuned
during dawn somewhere.
I wake, hummed to life
by the chill.
You won't come here,
always the connoisseur of rolling notes
and tingsha bells,
singing bowls and floating harps.
one wrong note beacons dusk
Where you're from.
It's like the birds can't sing
or the river can't roar well enough
to be truly heard in your land.
Might as well tighten the air
and burn it all,
a broken banjo
silenced by too much talking.

©*Felipe Roberts*

Sacred Love

Sacred Love, Sacred Love,
come and find we.
In feathered breaths upon surrendered plains of still quiet.
Pour your molten wax, and settle into the hollow bone,
the marrow of our mosaic keening.

Sacred Love, Sacred Love,
enquire upon our pathways
create in we a breath...of...of...eternity...

Sift soft my soul, for I have found my Sacred Love,
spirit merging with matter in rivers of exhaled
remembrance.

Sacred Love,
take your delights within this pleasured breath,
come and find we.
I am changed and renewed, remembered and called forth,
in the elongated mysteries of your invocation.

Soft soft my soul, o my love, o my love,
may your living in me expand creation.
O my love, my love...

©Aurora Sunu

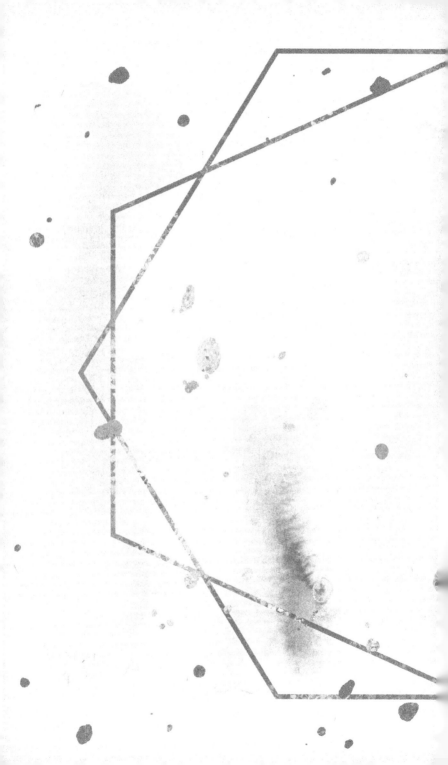

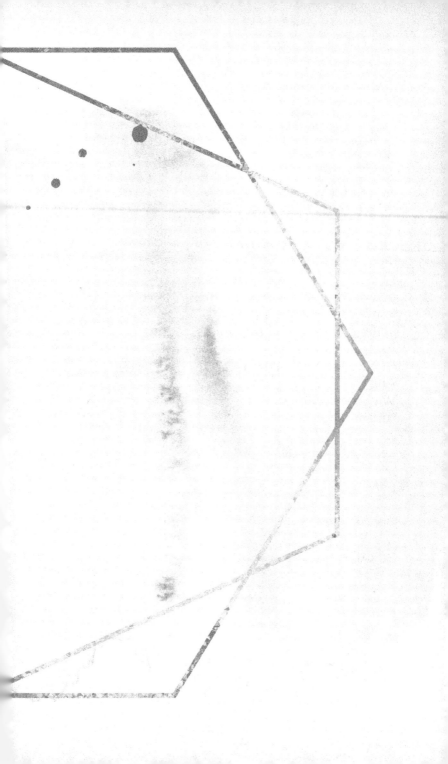

Retelling the Tales

I'll wait for you at the gate
Where our bridges cross the sky
and merge at this doorway,
our future incarnation.

I'll meet you at the end of one story
and at the beginning of another.
In the space between spaces,
in the space beyond the stories.

I'll pause for you, as you
And me, as me
With fresh eyes
And an open heart.

Let's tell a new tale

Pen a new saga

Dance a new epic

Isn't that what we want?

©Nichola Napora

Creating the Story

I am creating the story of love that knows no bounds
It's the story of a people who figured their shit out
We are not opposites, we are parts of a whole

When we let ourselves be
When we open our hearts
And let love flow
With no valve, no bounds, no filter
    'Cos Love can't be filtered
    Life can't be filtered
    We will not be filtered
We will become all that we are destined to be

I am creating the story of love
One chapter, one line
One letter at a time
It's mostly vowels
All *ooh's*
and *aah's*

I am creating the story
Our hearts combined
Yours and mine
Masculine feminine intertwined
One with the earth
and with all beings

©Heenal Rajani

This is where the wild reaches the eclipse,
the ravishing moon swollen in raw silence—
a smile on her round face,
surging the tides below
the power of her surrendered call is
found in the Nature of Love.

—Rebecca Cavender

CHAPTER 2

The Nature

OF LOVE

Hunter & Doe

Gently, like a doe,
she walked through the forest on a leaf littered path.
Maples and alders shed
orange, gold and rust.
Step by quiet step, deep in thought,
she admired the colors.

He was silent, waiting,
hidden with his rifle,
ready across his lap.

He thought she was the deer he came to harvest.
His pulse quickened
reflexes primed as he heard the foot fall,
felt the light trod on the earth in his body.

She appeared around the fir,
leaning and bent toward the creek
Her face lovely with a rosy glow from the autumn chill,
seriousness expressed on her brow.

Her quick agile steps showing she travels forest paths
often.

How has he never seen her before—and what was this
feeling in his chest?

©Deborah Wood

Nature Shall Prevail!

Have no fear
that we all may disappear,
as the litany of life's travails
plays out upon this earthly stage.
For surely as the sun will rise
granting vision to our hungry eyes,
indomitable, Nature shall prevail.

Though it may not be exactly
in those old familiar ways
to which we've grown
so comfortably accustomed.

Her seeming ceaseless cycles
of dissolution and renewal,
a cosmic *pas de deux*
choreographed into the habits of the moon,
who spirals 'round the seasons
in a rhythm that, like clockwork,
delivers spring's refreshing rains,
upon our planet's freshly furrowed flesh,
replenishing that torrid terrain
with a fertile flush of green again.

How thoughtlessly we've tread
upon the sanctity of her domain,
greeting generosity with greed
for our own short-sighted gain,
pillaging her magnificence
like a spoiled six-year-old
testing mother's patience
and the strength of her endurance.

But soon that day shall surely come,
(and maybe sooner than we'd choose)
when she'll lay down the law,
release her pent-up fury
and show us all who's boss.

She'll shake her lush and wild mane
and give her guests a toss...
in one astronomic show of force
she'll throw *us* for a loss.

For she has long-enduring traits
 (to which we have resigned our fates),
as well as an untiring perseverance.
She brings each passing day to light
without concern for consequence
to all who dwell within her earthly presence.

Yet unlike her most impetuous,
insidious inhabitants
who scurry about in frenzy and in fright,
she abides within her confidence,
with total self-assurance, knowing
she has all the time she'll ever need
to set her course aright.

So have no fear,
for we're all *born* to disappear.
There's nothing to be gained nor lost
in our brief sojourn here.
Though we may thrash about and wail
as empires rise and eventually fail,
the captain of this ship of fools,
Nature, in her wisdom, shall prevail!

©Jeff Volk

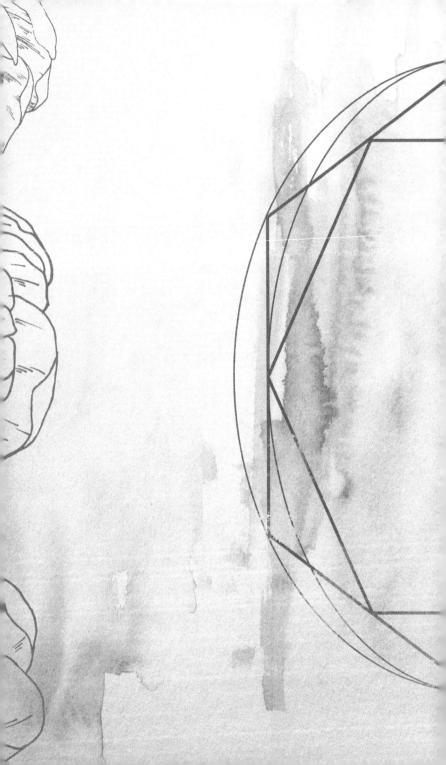

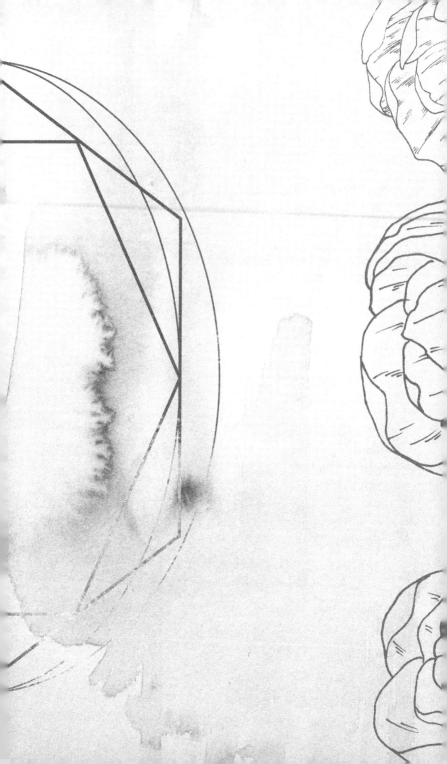

Touch

You there, me here; can you
sense my presence, feel my
gaze?

Does my ephemeral touch
bring about goosebumps?

I imagine laying next to
you; stroking your hair,
tracing with fingertips
your lips while my
breath lays gently
 upon your neck.

In this darkness,
are you as filled
with me as I am
with you?

©Lee Amburgy

Cup & Sword

My hands ignite the flame of love
And you are my teacher.

How do I touch you?
How may I approach?

Eyes lingering on your undulating curves
on the dips and peaks
that make up the landscape of you,
until I taste the tang on the lip of the sea—
vast areas of Creation,
its depth barely surfed.

I yearn to touch you
even as I know I am held.
I yearn to be enveloped in you
into the soothing crucible of your fire, forgetting,
forgetting that I cannot be separate from you
seeking the whole, of which I am already a part.

What Madness is this?
The wonder of it all—
the beauty, the struggle.
It opens my heart
already tender and longing.

How shall I now touch this light-filled grace?
Am I worthy?
Can I be filled with space?
The push and the pull of belonging to Me
O, how shall I reach you,
One who has never left me?

In a shared landscape we dream
of this Cup and that Sword.

©Nomita Khatri

In Love With the Dawn

I seek you
as the silk edge of night slips
from the paling horizon,
        as I look up into a mystery of silhouette
        and thin cloud.
You've been dreaming
in a sea of potential,
        full
        in your own meditation.
You take shape
        as you fall from stars
                drop
                        by
                                drop,
        forming a golden body of desire.

You're the first touch of rose on my soft sky,
you awaken new songs
        breathing fire into air.

You call me out of sleep
        to climb
                to wait,   to let the earth become my body.

You beckon from the East and I stir,
thirsting for your light
        like the buried seed.
I kneel on moss and stone
        lift my eyes to the diamond of sun
        on your hip.
                All the night's yearning
                        crystallizes and tips
                into the taste of this amber moment.

        I open my mouth to receive.

        This is how I learn worship.

You teach me to rise
        with all the ardor of being:
                iron and fierce appetite, bone and hard
beating heart.
        To stand,   dressed in light,
                devoted to morning.
I tend your garden
        and watch
        how the sun fills
        the flesh of creation.

You give me movement.

     My heart pounds for you, my body aches
     into the surety of bone and river.

You make me a man in your gaze
     I sing your divinity back to you.

You put the spark on my lips with your kiss,
     I swallow and catch fire.

     I am yours.

©Noel Tendick

The Air is Thick With Light

Heat, bright as a sun-torched gourd
(a drinking well,
deep with thought,
an expression of
your truth,
your surrender,
your quenched thirst).

The hush of silence,
a patient waiting for your words
(rising slowly like dawn
and this heat,
ablaze with your heart-rays)
generating fuel for us to
move forward
onward
toward
the dance of life,
entwined:
the center of your palm in mine.

You are the well
of my great dreams
of my assured tenderness
of my reflected hope,
awakened in the light of day,

I sip your words and
taste your love.

Come, wet my tongue.

©*Rebecca Cavender*

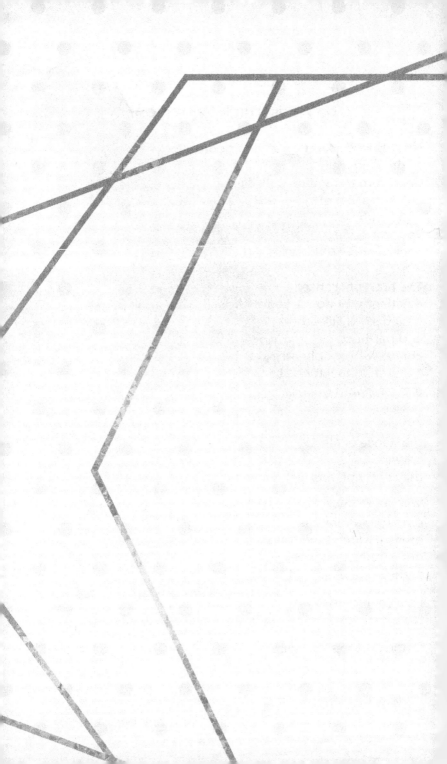

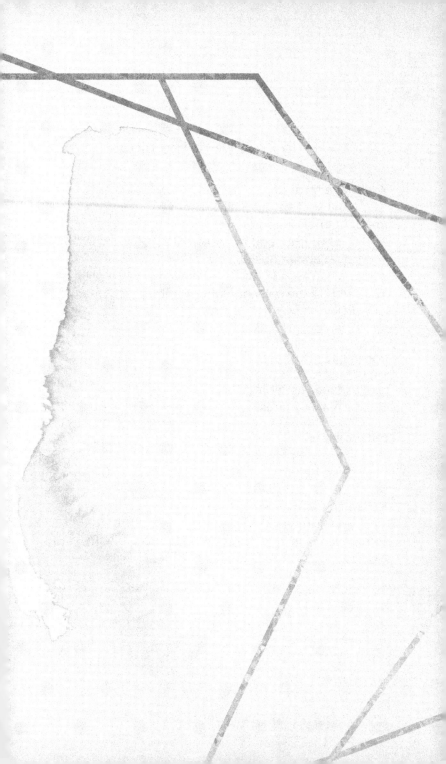

In Love With the Moon

You move through
        all seasons and all skies
messenger and creator
        of rhythm and release.
You hover above dusk
wearing a crescent cut,   allowing only a glimpse.
You feed on the calls of night's hunters
and drink
        an ocean of light.

Your belly swells.

You seduce the blood's iron
        making tides,

reminding us
        we are of land
        we belong to water.

You're so many words
        waiting
to be caught in cup,   poured out in ink,   whispered
closely.

You bind me to you

with magic born below
             waking.

You show me how to plant and harvest,
             to bleed and fuck
                  in communion with the wild.

I strip and move into your fullness,   let you robe me in
silver.
I am one
             who worships you in ecstasy
                  and destruction,

who welcomes lunacy   and cherished darkness.
My blood is a passionate madness.
             You have me drink all the wine   and dance the
fire down to embers.

You accept the sacrifice of reason
             on the stone altar.
You ask me to offer myself   unabashed,
             dark desire illumined in your glow.
                  You forgive
                  what I couldn't be
                  in the day,
                       embrace what I am in your night.

Every pearl belongs to you, every ruby,
            every tear.
You give the sky back to stars and
move into the west,
            for you too must leave the world
                    from time to time.

You draw brightness into dark,
            offer me the nectar of dissolution
            as you ease into ocean.

I set down leather and metal: the cup empty, the knife
sheathed.

I wade out into dark waters.
You take my ankles,   thighs,   waist.
            I lay back
                    you fill my eyes
                            touch my lips
                                    my chest,
            all my love is yours.

            You give me one more breath
            to say
                    Thank you.

©Noel Tendick

Your Light Ignites a Burning Flame

bright on the lips of the water
wave after wave
you erupt
an explosion of love
an explosion of desire.

I hear you come in the night
stars kiss you
the moon bows.

You taste like memory
a forgotten friend
ready to be remembered.

I need you. Here.
In the grips of my fingers
the grips of my womb
the grips of my blood.

I need you. Here.
So I can
call you home to my heart.

Oh, your light ignites my burning flame.
Come.
Come, home.
Come home to the sanctity of Love.

©Rebecca Cavender

Invitation From the High Priestess

Content,
I watch you
watching me

gazing at Mama Ocean,
moving with her from shore to mystery

I breathe in wave sounds

Join me
Say yes
Open the door to my water

Hear the sound of waves
Give yourself to me

I'll nurture you with my magical hands and
please myself while the
stars and moon make love to us

©Marie Mbouni

Warm Breath of Gaia (Mother Earth)

Earth
Your love scented summer breath drifts soft across
my salted flesh,
Beneath the Sun filled turquoise sky of your velvet
fingered mesh.
And I am lost enveloped in the rhythmic pulse of
your glowing inner warmth,
As your ripening seed heads crack, stand firm upon
the fertile earth.

Air
Tethered by a tiny warp you spun and carefully left
for me,
I probe and squirm like a bending bough upon a
breeze blown tree.
And the oxygen of love you breathe you share at
my behest,
Like the sweet breath that burgeons warm within
your swollen breast.

Water
I waft like ribboned kelp fronds swaying in your warm body brine,
As a tide of salty spume bathes my inner ocean heart and mind.
And as my sweet sugar soul dissolves in the wetness of your body tears,
I am submerged, helpless in your foaming swell of love and care.

Fire
Gazing transfixed, drawn deep into, your loving eyes desire,
My burning lust penetrates, smoulders inside me like a fire.
Spurts like the sulphur siphons of your restless vulcan womb,
Explode my salty love mast with its Mother Earth perfume!

©*John Beckett*

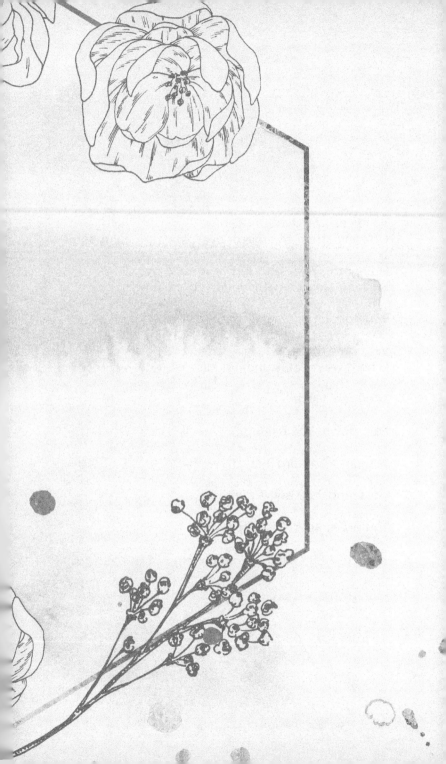

River & Rock

You keep watch at my banks.
Offering strength I mirror over ledges in calm pools.

I carve this river through your rock,
Snaking along a path we are co-creating.

You hold time. I make space.

We come together.
Where we meet is undefined.

You arch. I slide.

I dip down. You rise up.

You push forward. I crash over.

I descend. You await me there.

You break apart. I shelter you.

I churn and swirl. You hold me still.

Dropping from your cliffs I cascade and pull you in.

We trace each other's edges. Rough. Smooth.

The forests grow around us.
Nourished by my offering, held by your unfaltering.

At the estuary, we join ocean and sand.
Me, the water and You, the land.

We are always there. Joining the misted air.

©Nichola Napora

The Playful Hare

I am the tide that carries you
and the golden rays,
I am the sand that drifts and blows
as your body gently sways.

I am the cloud that floats on by
and the Faerie Queen,
I am the soothing air you breathe
as your body rests serene.

I am the Sun that lights your day
and the playful hare,
I am the warmth of infinite trust
and a mayfly with no care.

I am the rain which softly falls
upon your mystic blue,
I am the early morning mist
that gently soaks you through.

I am the breeze that strokes your skin
and the dancing bower bird
I am the wind that tugs your heart
and sings the sweetest words.

I am the sea that silver gives
and the trout that swims so deep,
I am the ocean of your mind
when you are fast asleep.

And you
You are the living goddess true
a sensuous perfect being,
you are the early morning dew
a spirit sense all seeing.

©John Beckett

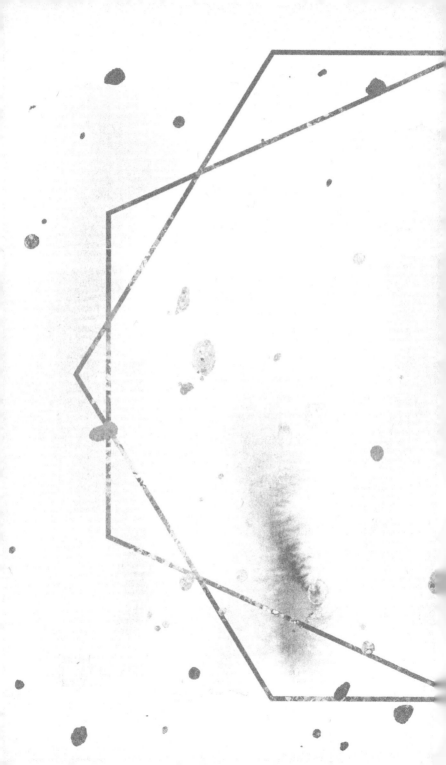

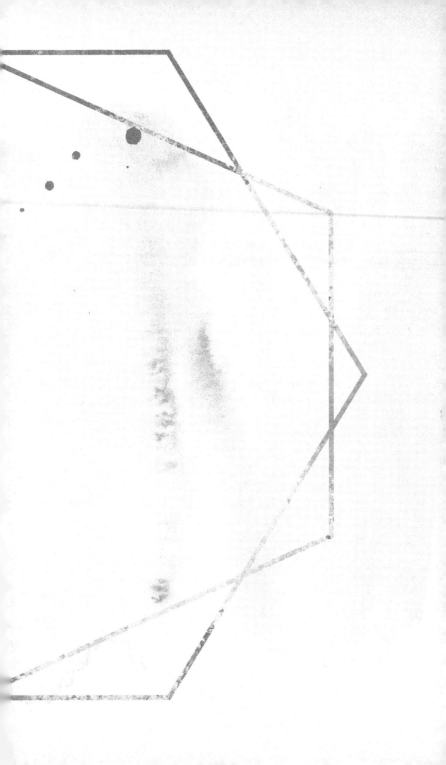

Welcoming the Masculine Home

I am the yoni, the portal to all that is
    the gateway to freedom
    the unknown, the unborn, the unstruck sound
    the darkness of deep space
I am here always, waiting for you

There is only love

Eternally always, for you to find me
    to find the infinite within you
    to find the Universe within you
    the power that comes from within
The knowingness that there is no separation

There is only love

How I have missed this empowered place of you
    I have missed the sweet nectar of your open heart
    a blossoming flower, petals opened to the light
    singing deep embrace
An Interwoven tango of souls

There is only love

Beloved Masculine, I hear the music of your lingam
            pouring from your heart portal,
            on a journey to ecstasy,
            from the stars to Gaia, the sun and the moon
I celebrate you
I anoint you
I honor you and receive you

I welcome you home

©*Marie Mbouni*

No Promises, No Lies

Gone are the idle promises,
Of love's desires from my youth,
I am hollowed and gentler now.

I come here in silence, my love,
Something has broken free of me,
Or rather, I am broken and free.

My love does not feel boundaries,
It is whole and it seeks for you,
Like roots reaching for falling rain.

It is peaceful here in the center,
Far away from all fears and loss,
Come, take my hand and follow me.

We will live here quietly and always,
While our bodies and minds run free,
Living out their own destinies.

I have nothing rich to offer,
But if you will take them from me,
I will give you my heart and time.

Give me a chance to share with you,
This ordinary, uncaused joy,
Arising endlessly from love.

We will stand shoulder to shoulder,
Inseparable from our shadows,
Unfolding life together.

If the time comes when you must go,
Know that freedom was always yours,
My love is a cage without walls.

©Sanjay Sabnani

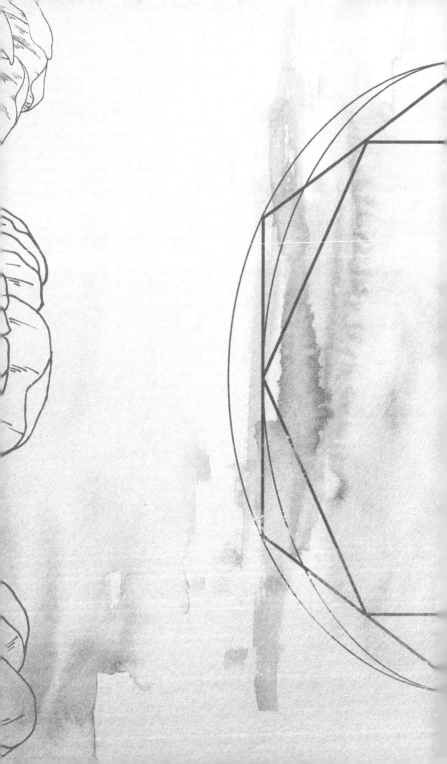

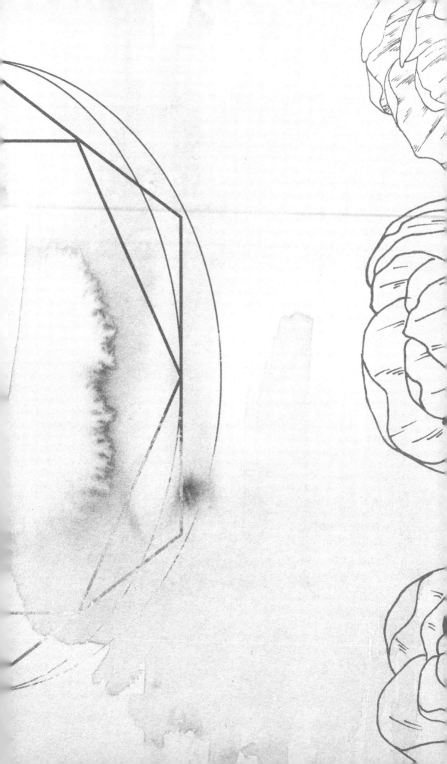

Speaking Wholeness

Am I not
the sacred waters
smoothing over
hardened edges
swirling into oneness
beneath the open sky?

Are you not
the molten lava
moving, flowing,
cooling, hardening,
bringing death
then birthing vibrant life?

We are the breath
of him/her, both/and,
one and all
bound together
by ecstatic creation.

You and I
we, mirrors
we, lovers
hand in hand
speak wholeness,
speak oneness,
speak life.

©Reese Leyva

In the Darkness Under Mountains

I ache to rise
in rivers of fire
cupping destruction,

cracking open

knowing you will come,

knowing you will fall as prisms
pregnant with light
cooling into stone
grinding in time
to nourish
the first seeds in soil;

knowing you will crash as ocean
onto jagged shores
and break them down into
gentle slopes of sand.

I exhale sparks
as you breathe in stars.
I push green shoots
toward your open sun heart.
We give ourselves
to the tumbling, twirling embrace
of atoms and galaxies,
pulled close as kiss at dawn,
thrust wide as sky enveloped in night.

©Noel Tendick

My love,
Clear the veils and blow away the mist.
Take my hand as I anoint you with a kiss.

Let us find our way to one another
through the Song of Love.

—Rebecca Cavender

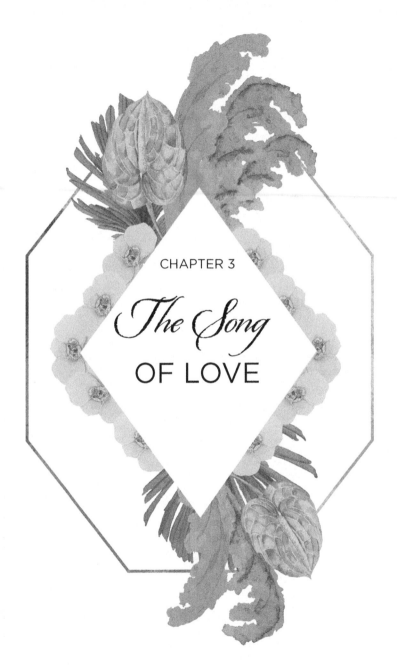

CHAPTER 3

The Song

OF LOVE

Birdsong in the Morning

Do you see it?
The ocean beyond the mountains.
Vast, turquoise and limitless.
Cradling your body.
A life.
No longer,
to be condemned.

Do you feel it?
The wind moving through the forest.
It's strength reassuring.
Pushing your essence.
A guide.
Forever,
delivering its promises.

Do you hear it?
The birdsong in the morning
It's words long familiar.
Nesting in your heart.
An ode.
To the years,
we missed together.

I do.
Your beauty and art is nature.
You are the elements, I crave.
Resting in my bones.
Your lyric.
Its gentle words,
illuminate my shadows.

©David Lea-Smith

Wind Songs

This is not the kind of love borne from
cedar-ocean-moss
or the scent of rain
kissing your cheek.

This is not lost in soft tides—
ebbing-flowing
emotional currents
changed by the hour,
traveling outside territories
searching searching searching.

No.

This love swallows the exposed heart
sand-dust torn,
made from eruption-floods
basalt-strong,
silica light.

This love nourishes the dry landscape of
any body that has been
over-watered,
under-heated.

It will suck minerals into you so ancient,
you'll hear the wind songs echo through your bone
rising to greet the sun-lit moon.

I'll show you
crags and sharp lines:
the way pain etches across stone,
carving new life
new dreams—
raw and bare.

I'll take you to the round rock
moulded from curved hills
—the desire valleys—
poised to receive you,
revive you.

This is the enduring love of shifting land,
free from broken ice, water and ash,
beating its drum
high on the plateau
chinook in hair,
moans that cut through rivers,
grounded in land.

This is the love that awaits you.

©Rebecca Cavender

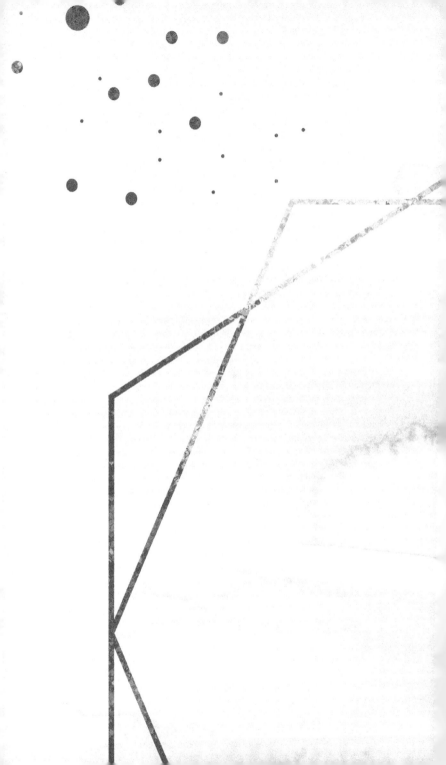

I Want to Sing in You

My hips sway to your music:
 the way you play inside my heart,
 strumming chords of a symphonic fire,
composed by your touch.

I want to sing in you,
 rise up your spine
 through your fingertips
 out your throat

a union without words
 only sound
 only love
 only grace.

©Rebecca Cavender

I Am Your Song

My feet feel a rhythm in earth
like a drum
like a heartbeat
pushing light into them,
into air,
drawing them down down down.
I feel you sway
as if in water,
your hips making waves
that come to me
one by one
composing a melody
of wanting

to fill my belly with music

to make my mouth a chamber of song

to pour myself out for you.

I follow, caught in currents,
yours and my own making,
both of us instrument
and composer.

My spine curves like a bow
you draw across your heart.
I'm yours in long vibration,
I'm yours in all surrender
of muscle into light.

My fingertips trace
the surface of water
as I watch our symphony
unspool in ripples and waves
seeking shore.

©Noel Tendick

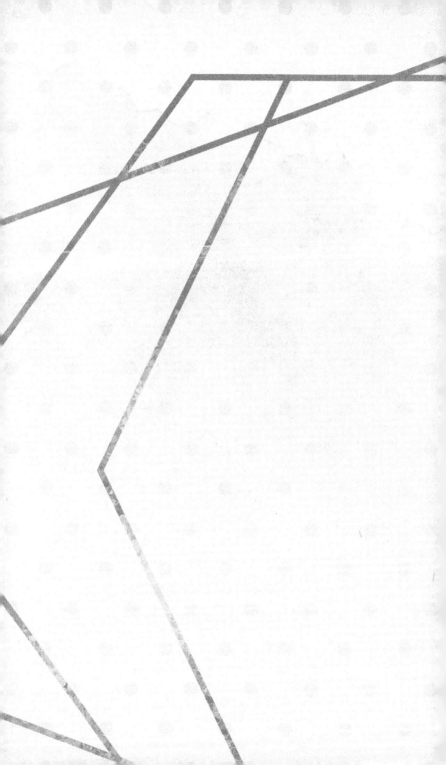

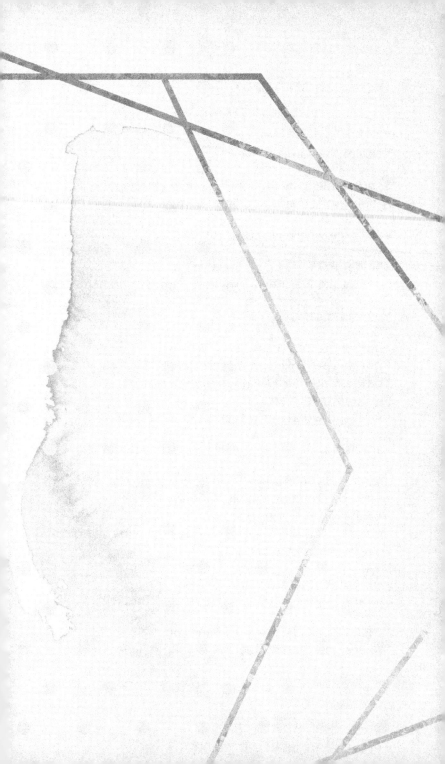

A Note

You are the song of love.

Sending me spinning in a cosmic dance.
A dance of dreams activated in my soul.

The place where we converge.

The depth of my being feels you as a pulse.
It beats like a drum in a rhythm of remembrance.

Your song sets me free.

You call me into the wild.
Into the vast unknown mystery.
So free. Untethered. Unhooked.
My cage splintered
metal and wood at my feet.

I am rising.

I can't see you but I feel you holding me. Caressing me.
Softly, deliberately, wholly, tenderly.
Reaching for your touch.
You to surrender. To let myself be held without holding.
To refrain from reaching.

Without speaking, I hear you say:
We are connected. Our senses in synchronicity.

When I let go, so do you. I hear you.
We are one. Singing the sweet song of love.

©Nichola Napora

Song of Love

You are the song of love.
A song as wistful as a whisper,
scintillating as sound itself.
Enticing, no... commanding me
to turn my head your way,

to stare, as if enraptured
by sirens' ceaseless symphonies—
unique unto this moment, yet somehow
so familiar that I feel as if I surely
must have dreamt them up myself!

Be still, my sweet encumbrance,
that I might hear you deep within my soul.
Your breath, the pulsing of the planet
your heartbeat, the twinkling of stars.

The rhythm of your breathing,
as entrancing as an ancient incantation,
captures my imagination like a spell—
while your quivering tongue articulates
the most delicate arpeggios of desire.

Your half-closed eyes call out to me
calling me to attention,
to attend to your slightly parted lips—
which glisten so invitingly,
offering their unsung ballad
of persuasion.

What more is there to do,
than to surrender?
Dismiss those stolid sentinels
those staunch and steadfast bodyguards
who keep us safe and firmly bound,
securely sequestered
within our separate skins.

Relax your anxious vigilance,
yield gently to that
sweet, seductive snare
that has but one objective—
to free you from the lair,
so you might lose yourself
in me, myself in you...
that we may flow along together
spinning silent melodies.

Like silken eddies, intertwined,
in sacred union, our souls align.
You close your eyes
I seal my ears
our hearts implode
we harmonize.

And merging slowly into one
magnificent moment out of time,
our song of love, forever sung,
serenades the music of the spheres.

Till finally that stubborn sense
of you and me, at last—
releases is persistent grasp
and graciously, just disappears.

©Jeff Volk

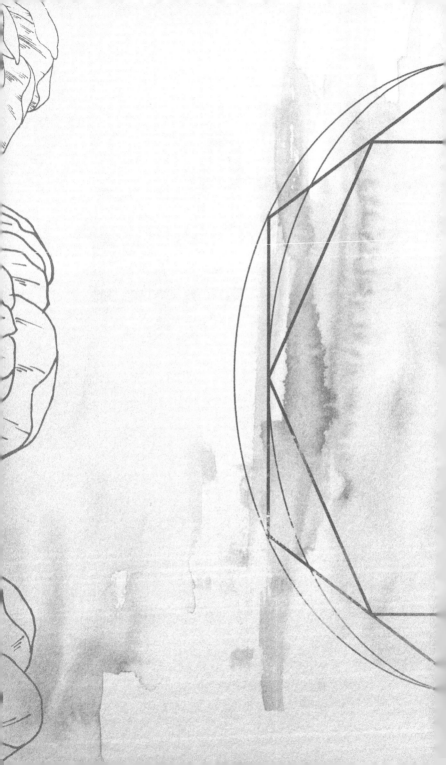

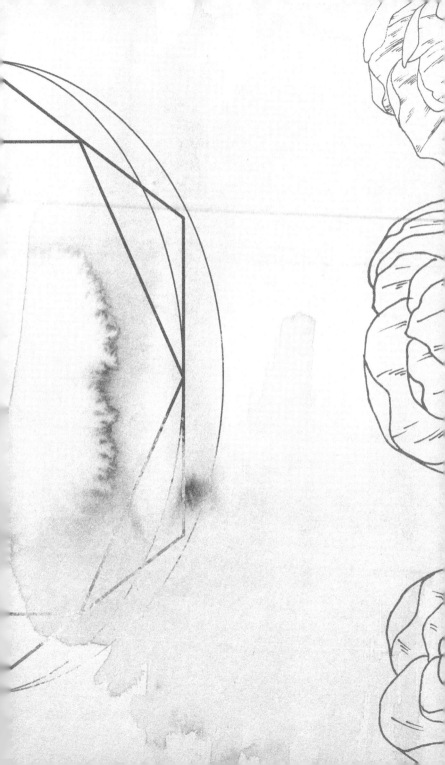

Two Minutes

I want to hold you
I want to admire you
I want to comfort you

I want to be with you
I want to nurture you
I want to play with you

For just two minutes
I want to love you

In silence

©*John Beckett*

My Beloved

I give myself to you
an open heart song
a true lover's journey
a blessed w-holy union.

In your eyes
I find myself

You are the second sun
inside my eye of Eden

We are here for the long run.
We are here for the deep dive.
We are here for the go(o)d ride.

Let's plant the seeds of heaven on earth.

©*Sarah Eden Davis*

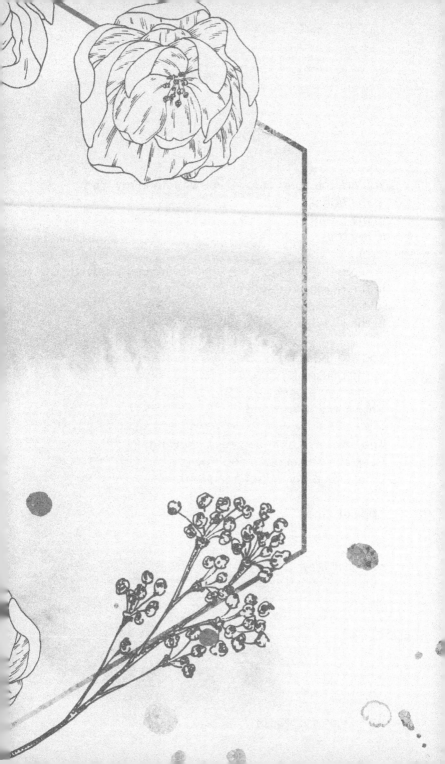

Speak to Me

You are the song of love; you vibrate in my feet,
In my bones
In my breath
In my toes.

You are the song of love; you vibrate in my sinew,
In the ripples in the river
In dappled shade
In the shadow of the rock.

You are the song of love; you vibrate in fear
In the pause
In the space between,
Between not-knowing.

The unknown brings its own knowing
Keep the vessel open and flowing.
I must keep my vessel open to flow...

Speak to me.

©Nomita Khatri

I Come in Silence

The song of love is silence;
listen,
In your bones
In your breath
Down to your toes.

We once were one;
knowing and being,
until we decided to unfold,
shadows of light and sound,
looking everywhere except within.

I am singing through your tears,
hear me in the scream of clouds,
unfurling dandelion seeds,
silently.

There is an unstruck sound,
speaking of an unasked answer:
Be silent my love, and open,
to knowing the unknown.

Listen...

©Sanjay Sabnani

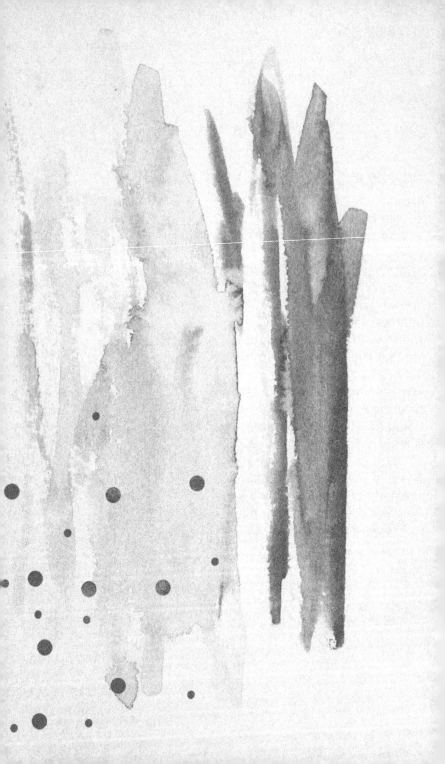

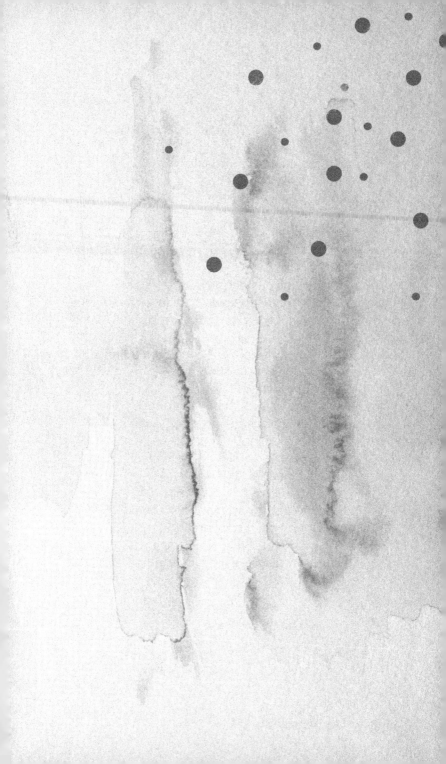

Words and Meaning

You and I, my closest companion,
may speak the same tongue
but we breathe a completely different language.

Your phonemes replete with oohs and ahhs,
and mine, punctuated by short, staccato sibilants.

Your words paint pastel portraits,
pink and soft against pillows of billowing cumulus,
while mine stick to the earth like mud.

What you might blithely call "our fine romance,"
I'd describe as "a few fleeting moments
enfolded between fond farewells."

It's no wonder that I find you so elusive—
your mellifluous melodies
lost in the discord
of my keening heart's lamenting wail.

Yet in this whispering moment of stillness,
where cacophony and conversation rest—
I come to understand you
and to learn, through your reflection,
those parts of me
I've yet to be.

©*Jeff Volk*

My Sacred Mirror

Divine grace surrounds you,
permeates your cells, your thoughts—
your voice and

I hear your soul's song
tuned to the music of the spheres,
true and clear

Your true beauty radiates,
born from your open heart
pouring forth Mother's ocean
of infinite wisdom

We are rays of light emanating forth
aligned in our highest purpose
right here, right now:

      I see who you truly are—
      my sacred mirror
      a holy union

I will shine for you,
lit by the
inextinguishable home torch

There is no sweeter taste
than this nectar of true love

      (We are sugar
      dissolving on the Goddess' tongue.)

©*Sarah Eden Davis*

When Love Happened

That day on the veranda, the island lush,
your hair, one dark cloud amongst the white.

We spoke of forever,
until the silence became too much.

Tendrils seemed to climb out of and into you:
you were the jungle and I feared fully losing you.

Something loud happened and I was back,
falling quickly into your smiling eyes.

The parrots rose into the sky at once,
like a thousand green hallelujahs.

We did not move
—we could not have moved—
yet every part of me
was dancing with you.

©Sanjay Sabnani

Oh, the Dance!

Weary lines reveal the folds of wisdom
written in the stars that dance within your eyes

The silence that rested upon my lips—
no truth could ever be heard
not a whisper, yet a sweetness that lingered

It was my heart song:
chords tuned for rhythmic play
the longing for your fingers
combing through my hair

And I stood. Waiting
as raindrops danced
upon my naked skin
dampening the fire
long ago ignited.

All the while, I danced that dance along with you
my sweet beloved

*(How could we (or I) ever doubted
the vines that entangle us?)*

©Dianne Chalifour

It's a new dawn:
Time has broken and you've entered my heart.
Together, we bow in sweet communion.
We give thanks to the rapture of our collective Revolution of Love.

—Rebecca Cavender

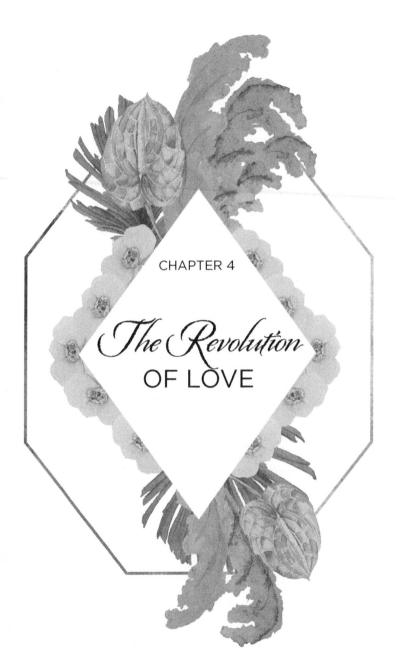

CHAPTER 4

The Revolution
OF LOVE

Yearning to be Whole

I am creating the story of Love.
From strength that shines through simple,
solid, fluid and gentle.

A truth-filled creation this,
Seen with the eye that sits
In heart and womb
Intimate and eagle-eyed
Roaming the landscape of my body and mind.

Trusting that the glow will
Suffuse the darkness with its steady, soft gaze.
To seek, to cradle, to listen, to embrace
To foster, to flourish and mold with grace.

Oh! How deeply we seek the marrow in our bones
The juice of life and nourishing rootedness
Yearning for what is fleeting and timidly held
Yet the story I am creating, is the story of a love
strongly felt.

©Nomita Khatri

The One I Can't Live Without

I have a need.

A deep insatiable yearning
that *nothing* of this earth can fulfill.

Yet I'm bound to this world
through my love of form,
and my fascination
with an ever-changing sea
of stimulation.

Washed about by waves of turbulent attraction,
only to be tossed asunder by the inevitable...
dissatisfaction.

No shimmering fantasy,
nor ephemeral beatific visions,
no matter how alluring—
can assuage this timeless emptiness.

Your most precious treasures,
even our moments of deepest bliss,
all leave me wanting,
hungering for more.

A life lived in longing—
punctuated by a parade of paltry pleasures
which only further fan the flames of my desire—

is hardly life at all!
Is it my own greed that torments me—
Never Satisfied?
Or might this incessant compulsion
arise from somewhat nobler origins?

Oh Light, great seducer of the mind,
deceiver of the senses,
cast no more
your long dual shadows,
between my eyes.

Focus...now...within.
For in a moment of stillness...
A moment, such as this—
All may once again be clear.

In the Naked Truth of Now
I offer you my heart, O Blessed One,
in gratitude
for a lifetime filled
with unfulfilled desires.

And for the million
savory sensations
You have dangled
before my lustful imagination,
to inspire ceaseless searching
after an eternity of apparitions,
which now hold no more for me
than this very breath, released.

For they've all served me well,
showing me, with poignant poise
and meticulous precision,
those idols I have worshiped
and how I've squandered
my most precious Devotion
upon illusion's shifting sands.

Focus...now...within.
This inward arching spiral
that draws me ever closer.
Closer to You.
Closer to my Self.
Closer to our eventual,
inevitable, Sacred Re-union.

© *Jeff Volk*

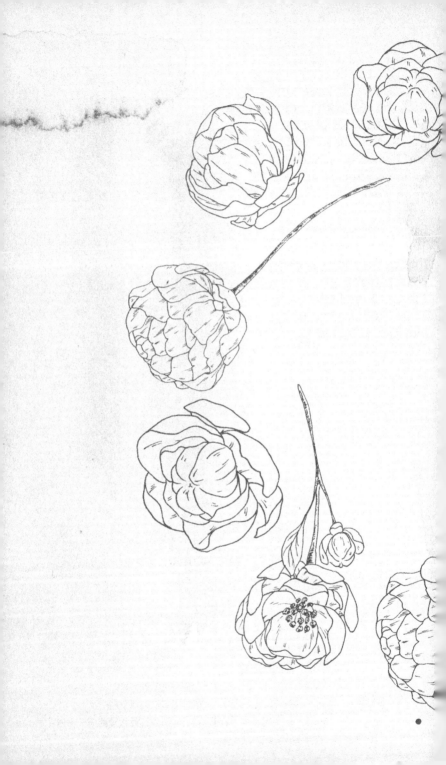

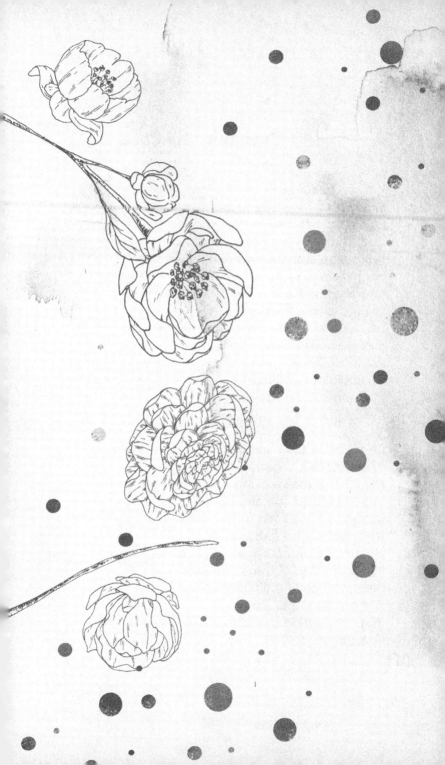

Revolutionary Love

We can become
a revolutionary story of love.
One that shifts the earth,
deep in the belly of existence.
A creation story of bridging gaps
our hearts to rebuild,
reformed by filling in the space
of time long forgotten;
when truths of sacred encounter
and precious union were known.
When we knew
we could not continue
the journey of forgetting.
Remember?

Re-member the parts
of our stories, together.
Remember the weaving of our humanity—
ribbons of triumph and tragedy
woven to alchemize
with these hands, aflame.
My open, glowing hands will hold you, again.
In the crucible of transformation—
the presence of my mighty heart.
The great mother speaks
from its burning branches
through me, to you.

And we'll rise.
With fire burning at my feet,
I stand, for us.
Bellowing the story,
coaxing it to come alive
across the veil of time.
Walk with me there,
through the heat of its thinning.
Peer through, with curious mind,
with heart split open
and stand, for us.

Over the veil I will rise.
You'll rise.
We rise.
Awakening in the domain
of invisible threads, passion red.
Heart strings, remembering.
Stitching bridges of connection beyond skin.
Closing wounds.
Old ways, healing with intention
as we travel the path of possibility
for a shared love so full
it bleeds over the pain of the divide.
Fusing us together.
Joined. United. Belonging.

Our linkage and lineage is human.
Beings with capacity to see beyond
seeing with only the eyes.
We are more same than different
when looking out from the heart.
We're of spirit and soul.
We are light born of the stars.
We are miraculous seeds
grown from an intrinsic wisdom
that does not favor.
We all have scars.

And with this honoring,
the shape of how I see you
and you see me transforms.
Form melts away to reveal
a prismatic clarity;
a frequency of compassion flows,
a new language is spoken,
and the story of us
changes into a revolution.

©Caroline Miskenack

She Came Before Me
[Lessons from The Feminine]

She came before me as hope
Doing everything she could to hold me up close with
warmth
She told me to stay
She showed me through openness how to cope, to em-
brace
She showed there is more to her pain
She cried, her eyes reinforcing the rain
Flash floods would become gore and in gore she would
bathe
She showed elegance
She rode her own wave boldly, with grace
She endured great distance through the stormiest graves
She greeted shore a survivor
She came before me as hope

She came before me as trust
She told me everything would be okay
She assured me I could be safe under her shielding
That tragedy often needs no reason but holds meaning
That pain is shared
That your feelings eventually become the world's feelings
That my feelings would be her feelings
She perceived me as one who once met evil
She perceived me as one who fret deceit
She came before me as trust because
She could both love and let me be

She came before me as freedom
Untamed and unbridled
She showed me adventure
She showed me to run wild
She loved smiling
She loved, she loved, she loved
Because to her simplicity was remedy
She kept telling me
My joy would look better free
She spoke my language, I tell you
That is what she meant to me

©Jermaine Anthony O'Connor

Afterwords
ON UNION

AURORA

And, so here, as you close a hand and breath upon the last page of this collection, let it be in prayer to the 'coming-near' place of offering; let masculine and feminine smoke itself round, rising to the cosmos, where creation will have its way—bloomed and sparked from the heart of the unspoken: polyvocal, and unapologetic.

Let it be an inquiry that transcends the shaping of masculinity and femininity gendered, an invitation into yet ever more expressions of love...

Love always,

Aurora Sunu

REBECCA

Just before publication of this book, our world began facing a global pandemic of the COVID-19 virus. In a matter of weeks, all of our lives became consciously intertwined and we remembered our interdependence.

Governments asked people to stay indoors and restrict their travel, shopping, gatherings, etc. so to be responsible and accountable to one another in efforts to reduce the spread of the virus.

I wondered if it was wise—or possible—to continue publication.

So, I asked the book itself what it wanted. After all, it's a living thing.

Into meditation, we went. Me and the book.

I saw an image of *Sacred Reunion* floating, hovering within a fire, but not consumed by it. Suddenly, the book turned into the face of a drum. Like a screen or a crystal ball, it showed the history of separation in the world. Story by story. The cracking apart of humanity from one another, from land, from animals, from the elements.

It showed, map-like, when all land was one and not distinct continents. Next, I could see how the earth looks today and was aware of the continued pulling apart and changes in land structure.

Crevices, fissures were exposed within our hearts and our environment. Then, a stitching up of the fissures and separation that existed—not a tight stitch, but a loose one so the cracks and breaks could still be seen as it heals into beauty. Simultaneously, it was as if the earth herself—and all of us—were skin being stitched and mended. Yet, the past and current pain honored. Letting there be space. Openness.

Openness for us all to be rewoven in a beautiful pattern together—land, sea, plants, animals, people...all living, sentient beings.

I shared this vision with Aurora and she mentioned embroidery and the art of *millefleur* (or a thousand flowers in French)—tapestries with many small flowers and plants. The tapestry of honoring nature and beauty.

As we restitch, reweave one another globally, I am aware that we can do this from a place of surrender. Surrendering so that we can completely receive love, union, healing.

From the fire, may we honor our interconnection and re-union ourselves to all living things.

From the fire, may we honor our interconnection and re-union ourselves to all living things.

Biographies

Amburgy, Lee

Lee Amburgy is a writer, poet, photographer living in upstate New York working through words and pictures to discover himself in the world he lives in and the world he wants to live in. The sensual, emotional, and vulnerable is where his art finds itself. He is currently looking to self-publish his first chapbook Four in Winter and can be found both clothed and not so much on his Instagram @Thsplldink.

REASON FOR SUBMISSION:

I am sure there are many reasons I can share the what and why of submitting. I know what stands out the most is my work mattering to someone other than myself and filling the insides of someone with feeling and emotion.

Beckett, Gordon John

Having worked in public services—police work, youth work, nature conservation and ultimately as a science teacher in a high school (1973-2009)—I took early retirement and commenced a new journey of self- discovery.

I now teach singing groups, supervise a conservation corps, facilitate a community called Norfolk Hearth, run a community permaculture garden and am the warden for a small nature reserve—Toll's Meadow, England.

In my spare time I write and perform poetry on nature and spiritual matters, compose and sing with piano and guitar, and run a small woodland management business.

I have been married for thirty-six years and have two grown up children, Sam and Kathy.

REASON FOR SUBMISSION:

I am happy to support this project as its genre chimes with my new spiritual journey, and the male/female mirror twist is genuinely of interest. I am exploring the power of sharing poetry and all its potential for good; I am convinced this will square a leap of generations with my ancestor, William Shakespear.

Cavender, Rebecca

Rebecca is a professional, intuitive writer/guide—and proudly autistic—from the Pacific Northwest, USA.

Rebecca intuits words and visionary guidance in a uniquely catalyzing and lyrical voice; they serve as medicine—a reminder—that we belong to ourselves and to one another: there is no separation.

When we know this, we can honor our sacred self-expression and share it in service to all.

This is where the starry-dirt we're made of tastes like bliss on the tongue of a volcanic eruption of love: an orgasmic recognition of truth and joy. It's where we create revolutionary stories—new myths—that bow to the world and spark lasting change.

Rebecca lives with her daughter, two dogs, and one cat on the traditional land of the Yakama Nation.

Discover more about Rebecca, her writing services, advocacy, and intuitive arts:

Website: www.rebeccacavender.com

IG: @rebecca.a.cavender

FB: https://www.facebook.com/BeckyCavenderWriter/

Chalifour, Dianne

Dianne is a transformational guide and leader within the healing arts, here to help midwife a more expansive, harmonious, and cohesive world, through her committed service to love.

As the owner of a wellness center on the New Hampshire seacoast, she offers products and services in her community that support and inspire people live a more soul-inspired life. Services include in-person and remote healing sessions, sister circles (so women can reconnect with their feminine body wisdom), and workshops. Dianne is passionate about guiding her clients to reach deep into their inner knowing and step forward, empowered—in their authentic expression—into the life that is waiting for them. She is co-author of the 2019 release of Amazon #1 best-seller, *Sacred Body Wisdom: Igniting The Flame of Our Divine Humanity.* Dianne enjoys spending time with her husband, three children, cat and her love of nature and quiet peaceful reflection time.

REASON FOR SUBMISSION:

Through a synchronistic conversation, Rebecca invited me to join this collaborative project. My deepest passion is to be in service to the healing that is underway between the masculine and feminine, so my answer was clear. It's easy to point the finger and blame where we feel our needs are not being met. To allow our hearts to soften, to own our projections, and open in vulnerability takes a whole new level of courage. I like to say 'vulnerability is the new superpower'. For it is through the tender, open heart, that deep healing can happen. I'm grateful to be a part of this unique expression.

Colombo, Satya

Satya Colombo is a certified Breathwork teacher and intuitive healer who has supported thousands of people through his private practice and community programs, such as Sacred Wild Mentorship, Soul Voyagers, and The Fire of Love Experience. He is most passionate about healing and awakening others to their true soul essence to fulfill their divine mission in this life. The name Satya is Sanskrit for truth, which he received from his parents through their lineage as Transcendental Meditation teachers.

Satya is committed to providing the tools and practices to empower each of us to be our own healers, and open the channels of Universal Love. For more than a decade he has been dedicated to fulfilling this mission as a healer, alchemist, writer, and teacher working in LA and internationally. He also shares his line of handcrafted, high-quality pure essential oils, Infinite Essence, expertly blended to move energy and spark transformation.

You can connect with him on his website at satyacolombo.com

REASON FOR SUBMISSION:

Humans are divided in the world because of how much we are conflicted internally and disconnected from our own true self. Perhaps because my soul work is to close those gaps and heal this separation, I could not refuse my heart's call to respond. Love is the medicine that brings us into the fold of our true soul essence.

Davis, Sarah Eden

Eden Amadora is a speaker, coach, mentor and spiritual guide. She is a featured author in The New Feminine Evolutionary and Sacred Body Wisdom. She is a master facilitator, archetypal channel, mystic and muse.

After 20 years of yogic and shamanic training, Eden found her heart at home in the 13 Moon Mystery School. She is now an Ordained Priestess, ecstatic embodiment guide, and initiator, witnessing the life-changing transformations that occur in her ceremonial spaces working with the archetypes of the Divine Feminine and initiating men through embodying the archetypes of the Sacred Masculine.

As a ceremonial facilitator, sound healer and prayer-formance artist Eden also enjoys leading sacred song and ritual circles using sound and voice as an alchemical tool for transformation.

She is highly regarded as a pure and seasoned "presence of transforming love" and raises a uniquely effective call to awaken our authentic selves.

REASON FOR SUBMISSION:

I am passionate about exploring the healing and deeper integration possible within our masculine and feminine essence individually and how this spiritual journey towards wholeness and balance can bring so much healing and light to our relationships with each other as women and men. I wanted to be a part of this very important dialog and conversation that I believe ultimately is the key to bringing us out of the shadows of separation and bringing so much true love and peace into our world.

Hawkins, Erin

Erin Hawkins is a bridge between diverse worlds. She cannot be placed in a box: She straddles the realms of being a devoted Priestess of the Divine Feminine while also being an awakened, Christed woman and leader in the United Methodist Church.

Erin refuses to stand for anything less than the universal truth that we are One. Simultaneously, she unconditionally embraces knowing that in order to recognize our inherent Oneness, we must acknowledge, honor, and respect the differences between us.

She values freedom and knows that we are at choice in every given moment; this allows us not to be defined by the experiences of our past, the roles that have been given to us, or the expectations of others; instead, we can choose to sit upon a throne of our own choosing.

Erin is a leader, redefining power as being the Voice of the Heart, possessing humility through compassion. She is revered for being a beacon—an ambassador—of graceful courage and strength, inspiring this in others.

Through creating a sanctuary of love, Erin supports others in finding their uniquely authentic and noble spirit, encouraging them to embrace it and live life sourced from their inner divinity.

While bowing to her African American heritage, Erin accesses spiritual tools from diverse backgrounds and lineages, catalyzing women to surrender to the unknown and be an empty vessel of radical love so they may bestow that upon themselves and others, in service to all.

REASON FOR SUBMISSION:

I submitted a piece to this book is because I believe in its vision, to champion the power of the love and of the magic that is created when the masculine and feminine are in aligned mutual honor and dialogue.

My hope is that the pages of this book make a deep contribution to the truth that is unveiling itself even in the midst of our current global and ecological chaos: love can be challenged, denied and perverted, but never destroyed; it is always lying in wait to reveal the truth of itself and to heal what seems to be irreparably broken. Love is our salvation.

Khatri, Nomita

Nomita is drawn to working with individuals and businesses sensitive to the world in which they live; consciously co-creating with others of the same intent, to imagine a different world, is what makes her tick.

Her twin interests in good communication as a graphic designer, illustrator and tending to the interrelated elements that make up a garden, led to an experiential understanding of the value of tending to the invisible web of vital connections between people too. Learning to listen and to speak where invited, what is often left unsaid both to herself and those she is surrounded by continues to be her practice. Though she never consciously set out to write for projects, having completed a Bachelor's degree in English Literature before moving into the world of visual communication, she found that her love for story-telling with words never dulled. Her passion for all things sustainable, led to writing projects, that has deepened her understanding of both herself and the world in which she lives.

The nexus of this exploration led her to the art of Priestessing, which is how she came to finding ways of exploring the masculine and feminine in her artwork and again as a student. She now finds herself in Goa, where she spends her time practicing Reiki, drawing, discovering neighbourhoods on foot and working on a Master's in Ecology and Spirituality.

Website: https://nomitakhatri.com

FB: https://www.facebook.com/nomita.khatri

IG: https://www.instagram.com/quillandfern/

REASON FOR SUBMISSION:

I felt "pinged" to participate in this project for two reasons. The first being the call to practice sitting in my body to listen to what needed to be spoken, however timidly, which I seem to do best when there is a clear reason to do so and a deadline to keep.

Secondly, as a mature Master's student a lot of my time is spent in my left brain reading and writing. The desire to feel the words rather than think them and learn to trust that what is being written, even as the voices of "unworthiness" rear its head and the stab of self-criticism makes its presence felt, is what I know I will experience and hopefully accept in order to make this submission. Published or not, I hope to be able to experience the subtle and vast difference in the two ways that I am being written right now. Committing to a circle of practice in which the ways in which we are being asked to show up are so feminine or at least what I understand as being in the light of the "feminine" seemed like a no-brainer. I now hope to use the method that you have practiced twice with us to regularly infuse my writing with space.

Lastly, (yes I have three reasons not two), I simply felt a tug, a yearning to write to the Masculine, which I feel I have only just scratched the surface.

Kujat, Krista

Krista Kujat is a passion crusader who helps women who feel disconnected from their bodies master self-love, trust and intimacy. Krista is the creator of Unleash Your Sexy, a 12-day self study journey that teaches women how to reawaken the soul of their sexual expression through small bites of self-care and exploration. Krista is also the creator of the Permission Sessions Workshops and Retreats, where she helps intimate groups of women connect to their true feminine essence through intuitive self-expression, sensual practices and meditation.

Krista's work draws from her immersion in Gestalt therapy, Family Constellation theories, Biodynamic breathwork, Path of Love theories, the Dalian method, Vipassana meditation, Osho Active meditations, bioenergetics and the Hoffman process. Movement modalities are inspired by S Factor, yoga, Djoniba Dance and Drum, Mark Morris NY and 5 Rhythms. Krista is a certified practitioner in Somatic Experiencing Trauma Release, Family and Relational Constellations and Femme!

Krista has been published in Sensheant Magazine and has spoken at a number of events, including Goddess On The Go, WowTalks and FemTalks.

Born and raised in Calgary, Alberta, Canada, Krista lives by Maya Angelou's legacy "When you get, give." She's a world traveler, survivor of typhoid fever, lingerie designer, dance fanatic, a lover of music, winner of a Silver Medal in Royal Conservatory for piano, winner of the Soul Making Keat's Literary Award and has a passion for acting, including her role in "Conventioneers," winner of the Independent Spirit Award.

To learn more about Krista, visit:

Website: www.kristakujat.com

FB: https://www.facebook.com/kristakujatwriter/

Twitter: https://twitter.com/KristaKujat

IG: https://www.instagram.com/kristakujat/

REASON FOR SUBMISSION:

Now, more than ever, I've experienced how systems of love, intimacy, partnership and patriarchy are challenged. If in the past we've made assumptions about what it means to 'love' and 'to take care of each other,' now both men and women are asking ourselves… what does it mean to love and be loved without the conditions, ideas and assumptions baked into our gender?

I'm passionate about the Sacred Union of men and women because I long for humans to be united in love despite the conditions we've learned and the pain of separation we've weathered.

Lea-Smith, David

David Thomas Lea-Smith is a musician and writer living on the Salish Sea.

REASON FOR SUBMISSION:

I'm drawn to this project as a way to recognize the importance of feminine energy in an overtly masculine world.

Leyva, Reese

Reese Leyva is a poet, writer, and mother to two young, inspiring children. She writes most often about womanhood, human emotion, self-love, and being a Pinay.

You can find her here:

Website: www.reeseleyva.com

IG: @reese.leyva

FB: www.facebook.com/reesewrites

REASON FOR SUBMISSION:

I see the great wound between the masculine and feminine energies of our world, and the distorted images of both in our society, and I love that you are working towards healing these long-lived wounds.

In my piece, I wanted to explore the concepts of oneness, and wholeness, within ourselves and in community with others.

Mbouni, Marie

Marie Mbouni, founder of Heart Leadership, is a leading expert on helping high-performing leaders get reconnected and centered in order to achieve unprecedented levels of performance, alignment and joy.

A bestselling author, healer and speaker, Marie's coaching is sought after by top entrepreneurs across the world. Her clients include New York Times Bestselling authors, CEO's of 9 figure businesses and more. With every client she works with, Marie creates space for them to tap into their deepest gifts and true power in order to achieve their next level of impact and fulfillment.

Marie's work is a reflection of her unique background in both Western and Eastern medicine. With 17 years' experience as an MD in Anesthesiology and a Masters in Public Health, Marie has extensive practice in Western Medicine. As a lifelong Intuitive and channel, her Eastern roots include robust work in Shamanic healing, as well as certifications in Sound Color Movement Therapy and Yoga to provide a holistic experience for her clients who are seeking to uncover their deepest truth and achieve a new level of success.

Marie's insights have been featured in major media like CBS and Fox. Marie is passionate about getting her message of love and reconnection with self to as many people as possible. She is the author of multiple books, including the best-seller "Reclaim Your Gifts". She is also the creator of the Conscious Creativity Method, where she helps leaders access their creativity in order to achieve more powerful outcomes in their lives.

A philanthropist, Marie is passionate about giving back and helping the world evolve into a better place. She has worked with the World Health Organization to control AIDS in Cameroon, and is an active donor and volunteer for Just Like My Child, Girl Power Project, an organization that helps save sexually abused children in Uganda, as well as the Pachamama Alliance.

Marie is available to partner as a coach and guide with any high-performing leader who wants to reconnect with themselves on a deeper level in order to experience lasting and holistic success.

REASON FOR SUBMISSION:

This transmission is about healing the wounds and patterns of separation, betrayal, judgment, abandonment, loss and mistrust.

I am here to send a call for women and men to stand in the TRUTH of transcendent love and inner power, within themselves first, and with one another. To carry "The Flame of Spiritual Love."

The union of the Feminine and the Masculine, within ourselves first, is an ecstatic Divine Inner Union, which must occur within ourselves first, so that it can be shared with others from a place of fullness. My intention is to open and illuminate the portal of liberation, an invitation to soften into the embrace of grace, compassion, forgiveness and surrender.

Miskenack, Caroline

Caroline is a creative and healing guide, driven by a passion to move energy through her hands in a way that heals and inspires. Her writing and art are reflections of her story and the story of many, both present and ancient. Her creations are informed by her own personal growth and evolution and all that causes her to feel deeply connected both internally and externally. Her creative work is inspired by the domains of quantum mechanics, metaphysics, spirituality, mind-body connection, feminine principals, holism, and a deep connection to Mother Earth.

Caroline is a certified Intentional Creativity® teacher, guiding others back to their hearts and souls in order to heal and empower the self, and contribute to the wellness of the world. She offers transformative workshops and private mentoring on Vancouver Island, BC. Caroline holds a Bachelor of Science in Nursing degree, is a certified Jikiden Reiki practitioner, and is a graduate of the Whole Health Medicine Institute.

Caroline calls the magical Comox Valley home, where she and her husband have raised three beautiful children.

You can learn more about her creative work at:

Website: www.carolinemiskenack.com

IG: @caroline.miskenack

FB: @carolinemiskenack_artist

REASON FOR SUBMISSION:

I was called to this project, I believe, before I even came to know of Rebecca. In my poem, I speak of invisible red threads. These are the connections that go beyond space and time. And as the Chinese legend goes, we are connected to those we are meant to meet before we are even born.

When I read a piece she wrote for a collaborative book, I fell to my knees. I sobbed tears I didn't know I had. I knew that I knew her, somehow.

So, with this I reached out to her. I participated in a writing circle. I was invited to this project, and I had to say YES. The theme is potent and important. We are of like heart. And to contribute to something that has the power to heal and challenge the illusion of paradox—of difference—of separation between the masculine and feminine is part of what I'm here to do. This is the work of the soul.

Thank you, Rebecca for being who you are and inviting me into this sacred space.

Napora, Jon

Jon L. Napora was born 10 minutes to midnight at the end of November in 1984. Born to the cold. Born for the cold. Shining a light upon the dark, for the light was shone brightly that night.

REASON FOR SUBMISSION:

Opening up about my heart and myself isn't easy. Even this short love poem is almost more than I want to share. For only I can truly protect my heart. Maybe in the future I'll once again feel the flapping of my dumbo ear'd heart. I know it's there. I feel it whenever I hold a small child. When I think of lovers of the past.

Napora, Nichola

Nichola Napora is a multifaceted artist, activist, adventurer and alchemist.

A Canadian equally in love with her home country and the world beyond those borders. Her family fostered her active imagination and her love for exploring off the beaten path. She splits her time between the foothills in Ventura county California and a mountain village in the coastal range of British Columbia, with her beloved.

You can find her seeking beauty, fun and magic while weaving dreams and a curious life connected to spirit, nature and culture. Her work in research, design and development of sustainable performance apparel and gear combines her passion for design, well crafted goods, community, being active and protecting the planet.

She comes alive among the trees, in water, around a fire, on the trails and the dance floor, and being silly with her loves. She thrives creating both in collaboration and in solitude. She writes in pursuit of and in response to divine inspiration.

REASON FOR SUBMISSION:

When Rebecca invited me to the project I was an immediate yes. The collective approach and the writing prompts made it a magical project. It's been an awakening journey to contribute to this book and I'm grateful to be a part of it. Poetry is one of my medicines (both to give and receive!) and I offer these to the collective for enjoyment and healing. Bringing the frequency of respect, love and grace into form was my intention behind submitting these writings.

O'Connor, Jermaine Anthony

My name is Jermaine Anthony O'Connor (I often publish under Anthony Jones). I am 26 years-old and have been writing since high school. I found poetry through my affinity for music and how words could move. In 2018, I self-published my debut book of poetry on Amazon titled "Reminders & Revelations", and currently working on my next poetry collection release for 2019.

IG: @anthonyjonespoetry

REASON FOR SUBMISSION:

I believe there is much needed healing for the growth and stability between men and women—and through the creative, curative power of art we can deepen our connections to each other. Greatness lives in us all, but we must first learn to feel it within.

Olsen, Stig Bronstad

Stig is a family father of six. He is an amateur singer and songwriter from Norway and has released two albums under the artist name "Digel." He moved to Canada with his family in 2017 and then started writing in English.

Stig is married to a wonderful Canadian girl; she is "the key" he is still trying to find. She is and always will be a mystery to him.

REASON FOR SUBMISSION:

In my country, equality between genders is considered to be a key to a healthy society. Both the masculine and feminine sides to an individual are important to understand. After three marriages and some shorter relationships, I have found many keys. I'm still learning when and how to use them the best way.

If my writing may contribute in mending the gap between the masculine and feminine that would be my reason to contribute.

Ranjani, Heenal

Heenal Rajani is a community activator who seeks to help humans to be more well together by holding space for conversation, sowing the seeds of collaboration, and believing in the impossible. A social entrepreneur, reiki master, dad, stepdad and poet, Heenal is co-founder of Reimagine Co, a zero waste community hub in London, Ontario, which includes a zero waste shop and free community workshops and events.

REASON FOR SUBMISSION:

When I heard about the theme of this book, I knew that I wanted to be a part of it. As a community activator and a father and stepfather to young children, I see daily echoes of the pain affecting the human species and the healing that is needed to bring us back into harmony with Life. Our words have power. Poetry can be a force, we are a force. It is our duty on this mortal earth to speak our truth, to make visible the invisible, to embody love and unity.

Roberts, Felipe

I am a father of two children. I live in Yakima, Washington, with my wife, Nikki, and my son and daughter. I teach 5th grade general education for the Yakima School District.

I write poetry, draw, and paint.

REASON FOR SUBMISSION:

I was interested in this project, because all I ever do is try and make a connection with people. Gender politics has been the cause of many disconnections, violence, poverty, hate, and misunderstanding. There is a long history of problems that could have been avoided, but rather than lament it seems possible to mend the fissure through any number of empathetic acts. In this case art is one of those vehicles for communication that can begin healing collective wounds.

Sabnani, Sanjay

Los Angeles based, Sanjay Sabnani is a meditator who finds creative expression through words and poetry. Currently residing in Los Angeles, Sabnani was born and raised in Hong Kong.

IG: @crowdgather

REASON FOR SUBMISSION:

Love is the only thing worth writing about.

Sunu, Aurora

Lover to my beloved, mama and home-educator to our three sons, each their own wise and wondrous magic.

I am a holy reclamation, weaving dreams as an erotic writer, threading warp and weft, a pilgrim of pain and pleasure—knowing that love and grief are but one wave of each other. I am devoted to the expression, invocation and erotic artistry of the sacred feminine. I am here to presence loving compassion and visions of value for the embodiment of the ecstatic feminine, healing sexual trauma, body disconnection, and the dance of the hidden soul.

I am training as a sacred sex, love, and relationship coach in the VITA method, as a holistic therapist, and daughter of the Priestess Presence Temple. My art is an alive invitation into the blooming wildness of soul's essence, so that we might enter the mystery, walking our living ripe, woken with love, encouraging us to each be the art that we came here to be.

IG: @aurora.sunu

REASON FOR SUBMISSION:

I wanted to offer into this project because I have known the wreckage and desecration of the loss of the sacred feminine, AND I am blessed to know the awakening of soul that a loving sacred union can heal. It is bliss to bathe in poetry that explores the dynamics and reciprocity that sacred union can give life to.

Tendick, Noel

My first poem was a love poem, filled with all the anguished yearning of a 10-year-old. I've been writing love poems ever since, learning from that anguish and yearning, from the sharp edges and sublime moments, how to love the world more and more.

I make my love manifest in my professional practice of photography, where I get to honor light and angles of perception. I am also an ordained minister, writing and performing ceremony, and offering spiritual healing in private practice. I'm grateful to roam around the Pacific Northwest, trail running, training in Aikido, hiking the Columbia River Gorge.

Most nights I lay my head down in Portland, Oregon, where I'm in love with every drop of water. I'm constantly moved and inspired by my community of friends, my partner, my cat, my dreams, and my time in Great Nature.

Websites: revbluesky.com, noeltendickphotography.com, noeltendick.
com

IG: @revbluesky

REASON FOR SUBMISSION:

I've given most of life to the work of supporting healing: forests and rivers and oceans; people in physical, emotional, spiritual pain. There is much out of balance in the world as we presently know it, great fires burning, great storms brewing. So much separation, alienation, wounding. So we open our hearts to being broken, and in that brokenness providing company and solace and salve.

This anthology approaches one of the most fundamental imbalances, the one between the Divine Feminine and the Divine Masculine; two forces which, in their brightest lights, feed and honor and worship and love one another.

This anthology is an act of love and healing, a spark to illuminate that brightest light.

Volk, Jeff

Jeff Volk is a poet, producer and publisher who, for over three decades, has popularized the science of Cymatics, a fascinating study that scientifically demonstrates how audible sound can create harmonic, geometric patterns found in complex life forms, patterns that also appear throughout the sacred art and architecture of the world's great Wisdom Traditions. In the mid-80's, he produced a series of videos based on Dr. Hans Jenny's experiments with Cymatics, and in 2001, he re-issued Dr. Jenny's groundbreaking books (Cymatics, Vols. I & II). In 2006, he published an English language edition of Water Sound Images, by the contemporary German photographer, philosopher and Cymatics researcher, Alexander Lauterwasser.

Volk's 1992 documentary, *Of Sound Mind and Body: Music and Vibrational Healing,* won the Hartley Film Award through the Institute of Noetic Sciences. Its phenomenal success inspired him to produce The International Sound Colloquium, the premier conference exploring the power of sacred sound and healing music. He has collaborated with artists, composers, musicians, researchers and scientists worldwide, and has participated in, and co-produced various international conferences on Cymatics and related subjects.

Over the years, Jeff has distilled this wealth of experience into multimedia presentations and feature articles that have been presented and published worldwide. His energetic, engaging and often extemporaneous "lectures" articulate how the same dynamics of unseen forces, made visible in the realms of physics by Cymatics, are also at play subjectively, in our personal lives. His work spans a wide range of topics, always seeking to offer an expansive perspective that integrates the disparate…in ways that only poetry can.

Further information and several short video clips, may be found at www. cymaticsource.com

REASON FOR SUBMISSION:

I'm delighted to contribute my musings to this collective expression of sensitive self-awareness and inspired exploration. Over the course of many years of observation and contemplation, I've come to recognize that much of the strife that is so evident in our world at large is but the outer expression of the same inner malady. Whether it be the abuse and exploitation of the vulnerable (so often foisted upon children and women, especially those dependant and impoverished), or our disregard for the sanctity of the refulgent, abundant and elegant creation that sustains us (Nature, Gaia, Mother Earth), both are predicated on a lack of appreciation or a total disrespect of the dynamic balance of the masculine and feminine principle within ourselves. This has been very clearly elaborated by many, perhaps most notably in our Western, psychologically oriented culture, through the writing of Carl Jung on the anima and animus.

In my personal explorations, I've found that poetry offers a refreshing avenue to describe and articulate some of the distorted assumptions, fears and beliefs that underlie this antagonistic and exploitative way of perceiving the world—and our very own bodies—as little more than "stuff to be used up for our own, short-sighted purposes."

It's been a challenge and a pleasure to articulate a few choice aspects of what I've discovered along the way, in a manner that is immediate and accessible, and I hope, does not require too much abstract, conceptual thinking to appreciate and enjoy!

Wood, Deborah

Deborah Woods is a massage therapist and energy healer. She is obsessed with all things that create a healthy whole being—body, mind and spirit. She lives in a small cabin surrounded by cedar and maple trees and without electricity. She is a mother of two and a grandmother of two. She is experiencing a deeper love through being a grandmother. Writing poetry and prose was once a thing she did often but lost somewhere along the way and is now being revitalized in her life.

Website: www.empowerreclaim.com

IG: @Stonefeatherhealingarts

REASON FOR SUBMISSION:

I've been on an inner journey of healing the masculine and feminine within myself for several years…through sexual healing, spirituality and priestess training I choose January 1, 2018 to be a day to perform marriage ceremony of my masculine and feminine. It was a day sequestered inside my home, preparing, performing, and communing with myself. Vowing to be sovereign. Promising to be faithful and whole unto me. Harmonizing the masculine and feminine of myself.

Along with finding more about who I was through astrology, I became more convinced that I had a problem with aspects of myself that were being projected on men. I've witnessed my sisters suffering in relationships with themselves and their partners. I see men wounded. My heart aches for us all. In my work, I see the effects of emotional pain in the bodies of my clients and myself. It takes patience and dedication and every gift we have to heal the rift of the masculine and feminine.

I offer my words in humble passion hoping even the act of putting them 'out there' in print will help create the energetic shift needed to bring peace, harmony and equality between the sexes.

Made in the USA
Las Vegas, NV
20 April 2021